The

A–Z

of

CUT FLOWERS

The
A – Z
of
CUT FLOWERS

Gilly Love

VIKING

VIKING
Published by The Penguin Group
Penguin Books USA Inc., 375 Hudson Street,
New York, New York 10014, U.S.A.
Penguin Books Ltd, 27 Wrights Lane,
London W8 5TZ, England
Penguin Books Australia Ltd, Ringwood,
Victoria, Australia
Penguin Books Canada Ltd, 10 Alcorn Avenue,
Toronto, Ontario, Canada M4V 3B2
Penguin Books (N.Z.) Ltd, 182–190 Wairau Road,
Auckland 10, New Zealand

Penguin Books Ltd, Registered Offices:
Harmondsworth, Middlesex, England

First published in 1994 by Viking Penguin,
a division of Penguin Books USA Inc.

1 3 5 7 9 10 8 6 4 2

Copyright © Breslich & Foss 1994
Conceived and produced by Breslich & Foss
Golden House, 28 – 31 Great Pulteney Street
London W1R 3DD

Project editor, and additional research: Catriona Woodburn
Design: Cooper Wilson Design
Original photography: Nigel Bradley, Visuel 7
Flower arrangement photography and styling: Marie-Louise Avery

CIP data available

ISBN 0-670-85226-0

Printed in Italy
Color reproduction by Daylight

CONTENTS

GENERAL INTRODUCTION

Fresh flowers have been used for thousands of years for decoration, personal adornment, and as expressions of emotion. In 1950, a Neanderthal grave was found in a cave near Shanidor in northern Iraq. Not only did it contain the remains of a man who had died some 60,000 years before, but also fragments of bunches of flowers that had been buried with him. Analysis of the pollen grains revealed that the flowers included cornflowers (Centaurea), hollyhocks (Althaea), and grape hyacinth (Muscari) — flowers that are still popular today.

In the last forty years, the greater scientific understanding brought to commercial cultivation has created a vast, worldwide flower industry. Commercial growers are continually testing new and existing varieties of flowers to make improvements in color, quality, and longevity, and much is done by growers in post-harvest treatments to ensure that flowers reach their eventual destinations in perfect condition. In addition, improvements in modern technology, affecting transportation and refrigeration, mean that those countries with the perfect climate for cultivation are able to mass-produce flowers and export them to the other side of the globe (where they would otherwise be out of season) at competitive prices.

Today, a bride getting married in spring may carry a bouquet made up with long-stemmed roses from Colombia, lilies from Holland, orchids from Thailand, lily of the valley from France, and Gypsophila from Britain. What has become vitally important is the chain of distribution which ensures that flowers reach their destination in perfect condition. If they are kept too long, if the temperature is too cold or too hot, or if the flowers have been picked too early, the blooms will inevitably suffer.

Although not considered an exceptional luxury, flowers must nevertheless represent value for money. It is easy to be fobbed off with aged blooms unless you can recognize a flower in good condition. Most flowers should be purchased when in bud with a good degree of color showing or, if it is a spike-shaped flower, when the lower florets are open. Exceptions, however, are

The fragrance of *Anethum graveolens* is sympathetic with food, and accompanied by white *Phlox*, makes an appealing table centerpiece.

Gerbera and Chrysanthemums which are sold mature and fully open. A reputable retailer will wrap the flowers to avoid excess evaporation, which can cause wilting, and use paper or cellophane to protect flower heads from damage while in transit. Flowers should be sold from a cool environment, protected at all times from direct heat or sunlight. Quality flowers have healthy, firm foliage and stems, and any open flowers should be without brown edges or transparent petals.

Price is one of the most crucial factors when choosing flowers to buy. Although many flowers are now available all year round, some are still confined to their natural season and will, for that period of time, offer especially good value. Spring bulbs such as tulips, Narcissi (daffodils in particular), and hyacinths are available in abundance for a month or so, but are wildly expensive and virtually impossible to buy in, say, midsummer. On a special occasion such as Valentine's Day, mass demand is seen as an opportunity for increasing prices, and the cost of traditionally romantic flowers, such as red roses, often skyrockets. For better value and a more original gift, you can give red tulips which, according to the Victorian language of flowers, also symbolize a declaration of love.

Color and texture are other considerations to bear in mind when selecting flowers, and the incredible range available means that there is a variety for every interior and every occasion. Natural products in general feature far more strongly in our homes than they did even a decade ago, and flower retailers, recognizing this trend, are now selling coordinated bouquets of flowers to complement interior color schemes.

Perfume is also an important factor in flower choice. There is an irresistible urge to smell a beautiful flower, and it can be quite disappointing to find that the most flamboyant species often have little or no perfume. This is because, in the natural development of the species, color and shape alone have proved sufficient attraction for insects to effect pollination. In addition, modern cultivation methods have tended to produce flowers for their color, longevity, and disease-resistance, and sadly this often means that any perfume present in the natural species has been lost through cultivation and hybridization. Most cultivated roses, for example, have little or no perfume compared to the countless varieties of garden roses which are heavily scented. Growers, however, recognize the demand for scented flowers, and are now developing new perfumed varieties.

As a general guideline, many white flowers will be found to have a scent — such as Polianthes tuberosa, many varieties of Narcissi, and lilies. Indeed, the ever-growing popularity of lilies, particularly the oriental hybrids, is in part attributable to their fragrance. A couple of stems of the exotic "Stargazer" (an oriental hybrid) or "White Europe" (a longiflorum), for example, can scent an entire room. The perpetual affection for Freesias, likewise, is largely attributable to their sweet and heady perfume. Interestingly, it is generally true that the scent of a flower is most noticeable in the latter part of the day and where the atmosphere is warm and humid.

Having acknowledged that flowers are an intrinsic part of everyday living, it is logical that flower arranging has gained universal interest. The ancient Chinese considered it an art form, and many of their basic principles are still recognized today. The Chinese believed that flowers should be arranged using only two or three harmonious colors, and that the flowers themselves should also be restricted to just two or three types. This practise is valid, of course, but these days we tend to be more flexible. Certainly, a natural harmony of very simply-arranged flowers is favored over the tortured, static "sculptures" of wired stems which was the trend a couple of decades ago.

The hand-tied or "continental" bunch has become the most popular form of presentation bouquet. Here the flowers and foliage are arranged in the hand, carefully sprialing the stems to create a three-dimensional design which is tied and remains so for placing in a vase. The bouquet can be completely round and

Anthurium species

posy-shaped or it can take a more linear form for carrying by a bride.

Few flower arrangements or bouquets are complete without foliage, and as so many commercially-grown flowers are supplied without leaves, the production of separate foliage has become a vital part of the fresh-flower industry. A good and creative florist will stock a wide range of greenery, both commercially produced and locally grown, and in addition to what is available throughout the year, will often supply specifically seasonal foliage – branches in blossom in the spring, and trails of mistletoe and bunches of holly at Christmas.

To add to any home-grown garden foliage, the ever-expanding selection of tropical house plants makes it possible to find leaves or fronds to complement every type of flower and style of arrangement. Keen flower arrangers grow specific shrubs and trees in their gardens, and these might include *Santolina* (Cotton lavender), *Viburnum tinus* (Laurustinus), *Lonicera* (Honeysuckle), *Hosta* (Plantain lily), *Acer japonicum* (Japanese maple), and various bamboos, ferns, and grasses.

Foliage can make a dramatic arrangement out of just a few blooms, creating interesting shapes and providing natural support for flower stems.

Whatever your interest in flowers, be it as a keen arranger or an occasional buyer, a greater knowledge of the properties of individual flowers and of the availability of less familiar varieties will make choosing them easier, more personal, and more enjoyable.

CARE AND MAINTENANCE OF CUT FLOWERS

It is wise to purchase flowers from a reputable retailer, florist, supermarket, or flower stall, for however vigilantly flowers are subsequently cared for, if they have been cut at the wrong time, or are put on sale when too mature, or when damaged or diseased, they will be completely dead in a day or so.

Understanding the correct way to care for flowers inevitably means being able to enjoy them longer. After purchase, ideally flowers need to be kept in water all the time, but they can be left for a couple of hours providing they are kept cool. If they do make a long journey, they should be placed in a bucket of water, but if that is not feasible, then wrapping the stem ends in damp paper will help reduce water loss.

Once home, give the flowers a long drink in deep, tepid water after removing the lower foliage and trimming an inch from the bottom of the stems by making a long, clean, diagonal cut with a sharp knife. This provides the maximum surface area for water intake. Stems should never ever be mashed — even the woodiest ones. Extensive research has proved that crushing the stem destroys the delicate structure of the stalk, making it less efficient at taking up water and encouraging bacterial infection.

Flowers that wilt and fade quickly, and flower heads which droop mysteriously in a matter of hours, have been affected by blocked stems. This is caused either by air being trapped in the stem or, and far more commonly, by bacterial infection. To avoid this problem it is essential to use perfectly clean containers or vases, remove all leaves below the water level, and add specially prepared flower food to the water. A good retailer will supply flower food with your purchase. This special preparation contains a measured amount of mild and harmless disinfectant — to inhibit the growth of bacteria in the water — and a sugar, such as saccharose or glucose, which feeds the flowers and encourages the buds to mature and open. Adding flower food also means it is unnecessary to change the water, although containers often need topping up for those flowers that are particularly thirsty, and, of course, when the environment is very warm. Many people have their own tried and tested remedies for prolonging the lives of flowers, and these range from adding coins, aspirins, lemonade, household bleach, and even white wine to the

Ananas comosus

water. For consistent results, flower food is the best and the most economical solution.

The temperature of vase water is important. Tepid water is preferred as it contains the least amount of air — which can also block stems and thereby reduce the flow of water.

Finally, the longevity of cut flowers does vary between varieties. Chrysanthemums, Dianthus (carnations), and Alstroemeria are renowned for being long-lasting, whereas other flowers may only survive a few days, but all flowers will appreciate being kept away from extremes of heat or cold, draughts, or full sunlight. Some flowers are also susceptible to ethylene gas, which is emitted by mature fruit, vegetables, and other flowers, and which speeds up the ripening processes in plants. Ethylene is also produced by exhaust and household fumes. Some flowers, such as Dianthus and orchids, are more affected by it than others, although they are usually treated by the grower, wholesaler, or florist in advance, to alleviate the problem. Placing flowers in a cool and well-ventilated atmosphere where the levels of ethylene gas are at their lowest, and keeping them away from the sources of ethylene gas mentioned above, will help to avoid the problem.

Important Tips When Caring for Cut Flowers

1 *Do not allow flowers to remain out of water after purchase.*

2 *Trim the ends of stems, making a long diagonal cut with a sharp knife (or with secateurs on more woody stems). For those flowers which "bleed" latex from their stems (see individual entries), sear stem ends in boiling water for a few seconds to seal them.*

3 *Remove any foliage which falls below the water level in the vase.*

4 *Use clean vases or containers and fresh, luke-warm water. Avoid metal containers which are hard to clean and can neutralize the effects of flower food.*

5 *Add flower food to the water.*

6 *Avoid ethylene gas damage by keeping flowers away from ripening fruit and vegetables and dying flowers.*

7 *Keep flowers in a cool, well-ventilated atmosphere away from draughts and direct heat or sunlight.*

8 *Remove any flowers or leaves that wilt or are damaged.*

9 *If you are not using flower food, change vase water and re-cut stem ends every couple of days. Do not re-cut the stem ends of those flowers that have been seared.*

Chrysanthemum parthenium (standard)

PRESERVING FLOWERS

The tradition of drying flowers for decorative arrangements dates back centuries, but with modern techniques and contemporary designs it has been gaining a new popularity. Today, a wide selection of ready-dried flowers is available for purchase, usually by the bunch, and there are also many different fresh flowers that can be dried without any difficulty.

Until relatively recently there were three principal ways of drying flowers — air, microwave and desiccant, but the latest method is freeze-drying. This technique, originally developed for storing penicillin and blood plasma during the Second World War, is a commercial process, requiring expensive, specialized freezers, and it can take up to two weeks to complete. Individual flowers and bouquets dried by this method will reputedly last at least five years and, unlike other drying methods, will maintain the original color of the blooms and even their perfume.

The most common drying method, and by far the cheapest, is air-drying and this involves nothing more than merely hanging the stems upside-down in loose bunches or standing them up straight in wide containers in a warm, dry, and well-ventilated room. This technique is most suitable for grasses, seed heads, thistles, and those flowers with dense masses of petals or florets. Room temperature should not be allowed to fall below 50° F/10° C, and it should be noted that any humidity in the atmosphere will inhibit the drying process.

Apart from grasses and seed heads, foliage does not generally dry well, but many flowers can be air dried very successfully (see Appendix). Most flowers are best air dried at the middle of their development. For instance, Delphinium should be dried when most of the florets are open, but those at the top are still in colored bud. Rose buds may be air dried, but those that are fully open will only be successfully preserved by the desiccant method.

Air dried flowers are much more fragile than fresh ones and need very careful handling. The stems are often brittle and are best supported in florist's foam. Contemporary designs avoid trying to replicate the shapes that fresh flowers make and are usully displayed as tightly-packed flower heads in groups of one flower variety. This gives impact to the usually faded color and avoids showing much stem or foliage.

Microwave drying suits many of the air dried flowers too, but it is limited to those with shorter stems, since they must fit on the radius of the microwave turntable. Stems should be laid in a line, alternating flower heads top-to-tail or in a wheel, with the flower heads facing out. The microwave needs to be put to the lowest setting, and the turntable covered with wax paper. The materials need to be checked approximately every minute, as the flowers will vary in the drying time they need, depending on the variety and its stage of development. Once dried, short stems may be lengthened by mounting them on florist's wire.

Desiccant drying works by drawing the moisture out of the fresh material. Alum or borax can be purchased from hardware stores, although they are only really suitable for small or white flowers as the powder is difficult to remove. Silica gel crystals, however, available from pharmacies, are suitable. A half-inch layer of finely-ground desiccant should be placed in the base of an airtight container. The flowers should be laid on this, face up, and covered very gently with sifted desiccant until every part of the flower is covered. The container must then be sealed and left at room temperature. Drying by this method can take between 7 and 10 days, but may be speeded up using a microwave.

HOW TO USE THIS BOOK

Genus, Common Name, and Species
The following entries detail those species of flowers grown commercially as cut flowers (although it is possible to grow many other species of the genus in gardens and greenhouses). Although most flowers have a common name, and indeed some have several, these will vary between countries, so that in order to help international recognition and avoid any confusion over identification, flowers are described here initially using their botanical genus name.

When ordering flowers, mistakes can easily be made if flowers are described merely as, for example, "orchids." This could refer to any one of many types — Cymbidium, Dendrobium, or Aranthera, to name just a few. Similarly, what an American florist calls "stock" may mean nothing to a Dutch wholesaler who always refers to these flowers as Matthiola. In addition to this potential for confusion, some flowers have the same common name, for instance both Stephanotis and Chamaelaucium are known as "wax flower." Using the genus name for a flower will make selection easier and more accurate and may even mean you are given greater attention when purchasing flowers from florists and wholesalers.

Despite the importance of genus names, common names are vital too. Very few people will understand what is meant by *Asparagus asparagoides*, but will probably know exactly what smilax is. For the following entries, the most popular common names are detailed after the genus name and these are also all listed in the index for cross reference.

Introduction
A general introduction to each entry includes such details as the origins of the flower and its name, whether it is fragrant, and which other flowers work best to use in arrangements.

Season
The growing season varies from one country to another, but it is possible to determine a common seasonality now that excellent transportation enables flowers to be flown from all the major flower-growing countries to anywhere in the world. Many flowers are now available all year round, because as a crop finishes in one flower-growing country it will often be in season in several others. The seasonal description also gives some indication of cost, because although it may be possible to buy flowers out of peak season, the scarcity will be reflected in the price.

Available in
The choice of colors listed under "Available in" is a general guideline, since new varieties are being developed all the time and fashion dictates new trends — like the increasing popularity of bi-colored carnations and mini Gerbera.

Lasting time
Lasting time is probably the most difficult quality to predict with flowers. So much depends on how and where they were grown, how long and under what conditions they were transported, how they were conditioned by the florist or wholesaler, and how much time they spent in the shop or on the market stall. Providing flowers have been treated correctly and they are purchased at the optimum time of their maturity, the lasting time given will provide a good indication of their vase life. In cool, airy conditions some varieties of Chrysanthemum, Alstroemeria, and Dianthus have been known to last for more than three weeks.

Flowers
In addition to the color photographs, a brief description offers further help with gauging the size of individual flowers and flower heads. In addition, there is often a recommendation as to the optimum stage of bud development at which to purchase flowers. This is important, for if plants have not had proper care or have been cut too early, the flowers may never open.

Stems
The details under "Stems" give an indication of the shortest and the longest stem lengths which can be expected, variation sometimes proving great between one variety and another. Sometimes the length of a flower's stem has a bearing on the price; for example a large-headed rose with a 39 " (100 cm) stem will considerably more than a shorter variety.

Special notes
"Special notes" indicate additional important factors to be aware of when caring for cut flowers and advice on the suitability for drying.

CUT FLOWERS

ACACIA
MIMOSA, WATTLE

A. dealbata, A. longifolia, A. retinoides.

Acacia is from the pea family, although its name is derived from the Greek for "point," *ake*, and means "prickly tree". Cut from Acacia trees, it is sold as flowering branches, and has a sharp, sweet fragrance.

The species of Acacia traditionally sold as mimosa (although this has become a common name for most types of florist's Acacia), is *A. dealbata*, which has similar panicle-borne flowers to *A. longifolia*, but typically has fern-like leaves. *A. retinoides*, which is also known as "Floribunda", has thin, leathery leaves.

Acacia species

Season: December – March.
Available in: Yellow.
Lasting time: 7 – 10 days.
Flowers: Tiny petal-less flowers, in globular clusters, are typically formed in slender panicles of 6 – 9" (15 – 23 cm) long – as in the popular cultivar "Chenille" – or small round balls, as in "Floribunda". Numerous stamens give a typically fluffy appearance. Choose when the flowers are showing color.

Stems: Woody stems of approximately 15 – 24" (38 – 60 cm).
Special notes: Mimosa is sensitive to ethylene gas and should be kept away from mature fruit and vegetables, dying flowers, and excess heat.

Using secateurs, re-cut about 2" (5 cm) off stems to help water uptake.

Easily dried.

ACHILLEA
YARROW, SNEEZEWORT

A. filipendulina, A. millefolium, A. ptarmica, A. taygetea; hybrids and cultivars.

The name Achillea comes from Achilles, the Greek hero who was reputed to have used this plant to heal wounds. There are several varieties used as cut flowers: *A. filipendulina* has densely-packed, flat heads, usually of brilliant yellow flowers, and is useful for traditional arrangements in shades of yellow, or as a highlight to a foliage design. *A. millefolium* (common yarrow, milfoil), which has a shorter vase life than *A. filipendulina*, has wide, flattened heads of tiny white to cerise flowers. *A. ptarmica* (sneezewort) has white, button flowers that are more suited to informal designs.

Achillea millefolium

Achillea filipendulina

Achillea belongs to the *Compositae* or daisy family.

Season: Some varieties are available from March through November, but the main season is June through August.
Available in: Yellow, pink, white, red, mauve.
Lasting time: 7 – 14 days.
Flowers: Small, borne in 4 – 6" (10 – 15 cm) wide clusters, usually forming flat heads. Choose when most of the florets on the head are open.
Stems: 20 – 28" (50 – 70 cm), straight and woody.
Special notes: Varieties of the *A. filipendulina* species, in particular, are very suitable for drying. They should be tied in very loose bunches and suspended in a light, airy atmosphere. Achillea is one of the ready-dried flowers most commonly available at florists.

ACONITUM
MONKSHOOD

A. arendsii, A. cammarum, A. carmichaeleii, A. napellus.

These flowers originate from western and central Europe and Asia, and belong to the buttercup *(Ranunculaceae)* family. The genus name is derived from the Greek name for the plant, *Akoniton*. The Greeks used it to poison wolves and other wild animals. Because of its intense color, it is useful for outlining a traditional design, or contrasting with other bright colors such as those of the varieties of Alstroemeria.

Season: May – October.
Available in: Shades of blue, deep blue, and purple (although they can also be grown in gardens non-commercially in white and cream varieties).
Lasting time: Approximately 12 days, during which time the flowers will continue to open.
Flowers: Flowers with high hoods, 1 – 1½" (2.5 – 4 cm), on long spikes. Choose when the first lower buds are just opening.
Stems: Strong and upright. Tall stems of up to 40" (101 cm).
Special notes: All parts of Aconitum are poisonous, and should be handled with care. Always wash your hands after touching.

These flowers can be air dried, but any stem foliage should be removed first. Once dried, the flowers will be brittle and need careful handling.

Aconitum species

AGAPANTHUS
AFRICAN LILY, LILY OF THE NILE

A. praecox (syn. *A. umbellatus*), *A. orientalis*; and hybrids.

Agapanthus praecox

From the lily family, Agapanthus originates from South Africa but is mainly cultivated in Holland. Popular varieties of this elegant cut flower include "Blue Triumphator" which has clear blue flowers, "Blue Globe," and "Umbellatus Albus" which is a white form. The stem length and flowers are often sizable enough for Agapanthus to be used in large-scale designs. There are also some less common dwarf varieties.

Season: The main season is June – August, but some varieties are available as early as April and as late as December.
Available in: Shades of blue, white.
Lasting time: A long, cut life of 10 – 20 days.
Flowers: Rounded clusters of small bell- or trumpet-shaped flowers at the top of the stems. Choose when one third of the flowers on the cluster are open.
Stems: Erect and sturdy single stems of approximately 25 – 35" (60 – 90 cm) when cut.
Special notes: Agapanthus is prone to losing its petals, but this can be counteracted by preventing the ends of the stems from drying out. Re-cut them frequently.

The long-stemmed seed heads can be dried successfully for winter decoration.

AGERATUM
FLOSS FLOWER

A. conyzoides, A.houstonianum.

Part of the daisy family, and originating from Mexico and Peru, Ageratum is common as a potted plant and is becoming increasingly popular as a cut flower. The name derives from the Greek, *ageraton*, "that which does not age," and refers to the flowers of the plant, which remain vivid for a long time. The flowers have a faint, but pleasant, scent.

Ageratum houstonianum

Season: All year round.
Available in: Blue-purple or white.
Lasting time: A medium cut life of 8 – 10 days.
Flowers: The neat clusters of small flower heads resemble shaving brushes. Choose when the flowers are starting to open.
Stems: Short stems, usually 8 – 12" (20 – 30 cm).
Special notes: Suitable for drying.

ALCHEMILLA
LADY'S MANTLE

A. mollis.

The tiny flowers and the abundance of soft, fan-shaped leaves make this flower an excellent filler for bouquets.

Season: The main season is May through July, but can extend from April through September.
Available in: Yellow-green.
Lasting time: Approximately 7 days.
Flowers: Tiny, star-shaped clusters. Choose when they have just opened.
Stems: 12 – 18" (30 – 50 cm).
Special notes: Suitable for drying.

Alchemilla mollis

ALLIUM
FLOWERING ONION, GARLIC, GIANT ONION, ORNAMENTAL ONION FLOWER

A. aflatunense, A. giganteum, A. neapolitanum, A. sphaerocephalon.

Allium giganteum

The enormous seed head of *A. giganteum* makes a striking focal point in an arrangement, and the long stem can bring height to a design. Combine for a soft-colored country look with, say, Scabious and Eryngium. *A. sphaerocephalon's* flower heads, which are much smaller, have a faint smell of garlic.

Season: May – September.
Available in: Purple (*A. giganteum*), blue, pink, yellow, and white (other varieties).
Lasting time: A long cut life of 12 – 20 days.
Flowers: *A. giganteum* has tight clusters of tiny flowers forming a large ball, sometimes as much as 6" (15 cm) in diameter. The more pointed head of *A. sphaerocephalon* is smaller, approximately 2" (5 cm) across. Other species, for example *A. flatunense*, have looser clusters of star-shaped flowers, while *A. neapolitanum*

Allium sphaerocephalon

has white flowers. Choose when one third of the blooms on the cluster have opened.

Stems: Erect. *A. giganteum* has a particularly long stem of up to about 50" (127 cm); *A. sphaerocephalon* , approximately 20" (50 cm); and *A. neapolitanum* about 10" (25 cm).

Special notes: All types are suitable for drying, and *A.sphaerocephalon* in particular.

ALPINIA
RED/PINK GINGER, SHELL GINGER, GINGER LILY,TORCH GINGER

A. purpurata, A. zerumbet.

Named after the doctor and botanist Prospero Alpino (1553 – 1616), these exotic tropical flowers are from the *Zingiberaceae*, or Ginger, family. Grown in the Far East and Africa, the leaves of Alpinia are often used as foliage in tropical designs.

Season: All year round.
Available in: Purple-red or pink (*A. purpurata*). *A. zerumbet* has white flowers marked with pink.
Lasting time: 14 – 21 days.
Flowers: *A. purpurata* has a very distinctive, erect flower head. *A. zerumbet* has hanging clusters of flowers.
Stems: Cut from much longer stalks, the cut length can be as much as 36 – 72" (90 – 180 cm), although it may well be cut shorter – closer to 25" (63 cm) or 30" (76 cm).

Special notes: Misting approximately once a day with fresh water will help to extend the cut life of most gingers.

Alpinia purpurata

ALSTROEMERIA
PERUVIAN LILY, ULSTER MARY

Alstroemeria hybrids.

Originally from the cool mountain area of South America, Alstroemeria hybrids have been developed in England and Holland. Their wide popularity is due to the abundance of exotic flower heads on each stem and their strong colors and impressive longevity. They are generally used in massed traditional arrangements.

Season: All year round, with peak periods between June and October.
Available in: Pinks, oranges, white, lilac, yellows and reds. Often bi-colored or multi-colored, streaked, striped, or marbled.
Lasting time: If given adequate water, Alstroemeria have a medium-to-long cut life – about 14 days if kept in a constant cool temperature.

Alstroemeria hybrids

Bright *Calendula* have broad fleshy stems, and a couple of stalks easily fill narrow-headed jugs and vases to make a graphic arrangement.

Flowers: Irregular and trumpet-shaped, approximately 3 to 7 orchid-like flowers are formed at the end of short flower stalks that branch off a single stem. Choose when the first bud has opened and most other buds are showing color.

Stems: Straight, slender, and leafy, approximately 12 – 36" (30 – 90 cm) when cut.

Special notes: Both leaves and flowers are quite delicate and need careful handling. As the flowers age, the leaves will turn yellow, so it is advisable to remove any excess foliage before placing in water.

Althaea rosea (double flowered)

ALTHAEA
HOLLYHOCK, ROSE MALLOW

A. rosea; and hybrids.

Indigenous to eastern Europe and western Asia, hollyhocks have escaped from their familiar home in the gardens of Britain and France and naturalized in rocky countrysides. They are now commercially cultivated as an outdoor crop. *A. rosea* occur in both single- and double-flowered forms, the cultivated varieties tending to be double flowering. Althaea is synonymous with Alcea.

Season: June – September.
Available in: Pink, white, occasionally in red.
Lasting time: Short, approximately 5 – 7 days.
Flowers: Tall spikes of wide-funnel-shaped flowers (single-flowered) and rounded, full-headed flowers (double-flowered).
Stems: 24 – 39" (60 – 100 cm).

AMARANTHUS
LOVE-LIES-BLEEDING, TASSEL FLOWER, CAT'S TAIL, PRINCE'S FEATHER

A. caudatus, A. hypochondriacus; and hybrids.

Originating from the tropical regions of South America, this flower is named from the Greek, *amarantos*, meaning "unfading". The tightly-clustered flowers form racemes which are rather fragile and need careful handling. In the most common variety, Love-lies-bleeding (*A. caudatus*), these are tassel-like, and hang from the top of the stem. Because of their drooping nature, *A. caudatus* does not have a specific place in flower arrangements – but will look excellent if incorporated as part of a high, pedestal design. The other main variety, Prince's feather (*A. hypochondriacus*), has dense racemes which form erect plumes.

Season: The main season is July – October.

Amaranthus hypochondriacus

Available in: Crimson, pale green.
Lasting time: A medium length cut life of 8 –
12 days.
Flowers: The drooping racemes of *A. caudatus*
are up to 16″ (40 cm) in length, somewhat
longer than the erect 6″ (15 cm) racemes of *A.
hypochondriacus.*
Stems: 12 – 36″ (30 – 90 cm).
Special notes: Remove foliage from the lower
stem.

These are very suitable flowers for drying,
and, if dried with care, they will retain their
color for quite a while.

AMMI
QUEEN ANNE'S LACE,
LACE FLOWER

A. majus.

Related to the wild flower "False bishop's
weed" and the carrot family, these pretty and
delicate white flowers are being used increasingly as a more original filler for bouquets

Amaranthus caudatus

than Gypsophila.
Season: Most of the year, but peak period is
between November and May.
Available in: White.
Lasting time: 10 days and sometimes longer.
Flowers: Tiny flowers are borne on individual

Ammi majus

stalks at the end of each of many branches off the main stem, creating a loose, flattish umbrella of clustered flowers.

Stems: 24 – 39″ (60 – 100 cm).

Special notes: Longevity is increased if the flowers are kept cool.

ANANAS
ORNAMENTAL PINEAPPLE, RED
PINEAPPLE, DWARF PINEAPPLE

A. bracteatus striatus, A. comosus, A. nanus.

The exotic, pink flower head looks just like the edible pineapple, and it is usually surrounded by a rosette of small, spiky leaves. The rest of

Ananas comosus

the stem is normally bare, and as the whole stalk is consequently rather top heavy, it may need support in arrangements. Both the flower size and the stem length can vary considerably.

Season: All year round.

Available in: Pink and green.

Lasting time: 14 – 20 days. It can last up to 7 days without water, provided it is kept cool.

Flowers: Flower heads can be up to 10″ (25 cm) long, but will vary considerably. Choose when fully developed.

Stems: These will also vary considerably, but on average, stems are 16 – 24″ (40 – 60 cm) long.

Special notes: Suitable for drying.

ANEMONE
WINDFLOWER,
LILY–OF–THE–FIELD, POPPY
ANEMONE

A. coronaria; and hybrids.

Anemone belong to the buttercup (*Ranunculaceae*) family. Indigenous to the Mediterranean countries and parts of Asia, they have been cultivated since ancient times. They can be found in single, double, and semi-double forms. However, the most popular contemporary cut Anemone is "Mona Lisa," which is available in several colors, but is taller and has slightly smaller, darker-centered flowers than other varieties.

Season: November – May.

Available in: Strong, contrasting colors of red, purple, mauve, pink, white, and bicolored.

Lasting time: About 7 days, but sometimes longer if kept in cool conditions.

Flowers: When mature, the papery-textured, cup-shaped flowers, which are 2½ – 3″ (6 – 8 cm) wide, open up almost flat. Select earlier than this, when the petals have started to separate from the center.

Stems: Thin, 9 – 12″ (22 – 30 cm) long.

Smoky-blue *Eryngium*, bought fresh, will air dry very successfully if left in a vase, preferably in a well-ventilated room.

Anemone coronaria

Special notes: Anemones do not appreciate being out of water for any length of time, and they take in water quickly, so it is important to check water levels frequently. Keep them away from draughts, direct sunlight, and excess heat.

If the stems become limp, wrap them in damp newspaper and stand them in deep water for several hours. They will tend to curve towards light, so they are best kept in an evenly-lit position, or turned occasionally.

ANETHUM
DILL

A. graveolens, A. peucedanum.

Graveolens literally means "heavily scented", and this flower, from the carrot family, is often confused with fennel, which is very similar, but has longer-lasting, ferny foliage. Anethum has become a very popular alternative to foliage, though care should be taken in combining it, particularly with other scented flowers, as its strong aroma will dominate.

Season: All year round.
Available in: Yellow-green.
Lasting time: About 7 days.
Flowers: Clusters of tiny flowers. Always choose when most of the flowers are fully open.
Stems: 15 – 36" (38 – 91 cm).
Special notes: Dill leaves are very popular in cooking, but commercially-grown dill is post-harvest-treated and not suitable for eating.

Anethum graveolens

ANIGOZANTHOS
KANGAROO'S PAW, MONKEY PAW

A. flavidus, A. manglesii, A. pulcherrimus, A. rufus; and hybrids.

Anigozanthos means "plant with unusual flower." These bizarre blooms are indeed unusual, resembling the hairy feet of a small animal. The kangaroo connection is because some varieties are grown in Australia. (The similar flower known as Black kangaroo paw, in fact comes from another family, *Macropidia imperia.*)

Anigozanthos flavidus

Anigozanthos rufus

Season: All year round.
Available in: Yellow-green, red.
Lasting time: Approximately 21 – 28 days.
Flowers: Furry buds, 1 – 3″ (2.5 – 8 cm) long buds open at the tips of the stems. The flowers do not last long, but the buds do.
Stems: 12 – 36″ (30 – 91 cm).
Special notes: Re-cut stem ends once a week to aid water uptake.
  Particularly suitable for drying.

ANTHURIUM
FLAMINGO FLOWER, PAINTER'S PALETTE, HAWAIIAN HEART, TAIL FLOWER

A. andraeanum, A. scherzerianum.

These hardy, exotic flowers originate from the rainforests of Colombia, and are now cultivated primarily in Holland and also in the Far East and Hawaii. The most popular cultivars are those of *A. andraeanum* (Painter's palette).

A difficult flower to combine, it looks strong displayed boldly with a few stems of the same color or with a flower of a distinctly contrasting shape, such as Gloriosa. The dark green leaves are popular as cut foliage.

Season: All year round.
Available in: Strong colors of white, pink, or red spathes, and typically with a yellow spadix.
Lasting time: A long life of well over 14 days.
Flowers: The flower consists of a shiny, waxy, and brightly-colored bract called a spathe, with a protruding spike or spadix at its center.

Anthurium andraeanum

They should be selected when the flowers are open.

Stems: Longish, 12 – 24″ (30 – 60 cm) stems.

Special notes: Because they are tropical, these flowers are best kept at a constant temperature and away from draughts. Longevity is also increased if the flowers are misted frequently with water.

Generally they should be handled with care, because they can bruise easily.

ANTIRRHINUM
SNAPDRAGON

A. majus; and hybrids.

Reminiscent of English gardens, Antirrhinum is now a popular hot-house flower, particularly in the United States. Antirrhinums come in a huge color range, and the potential height of the flowers makes these ideal choices for modern and free-form arrangements. Combine with Alstroemeria, roses, and statice for a summer feel that can be obtained all through the year.

Season: Most of the year, but with peak periods between April and June, and between August and October.

Available in: A large range – white, red, pink, orange, yellow, lavender.

Lasting time: 8 – 12 days. If the stem ends are re-cut frequently, they can last up to two weeks.

Flowers: Up to 15 bright flowers appear close together along the stem spike. Each is about 1½″ (4 cm) long. Choose when the lower 2 – 3 florets are open.

Stems: Semi-woody and upright. 12 – 39″ (30 – 100 cm).

Special notes: Antirrhinum are sensitive to

Antirrhinum majus

ethylene gas, and should be kept away from mature fruit and vegetables, dying flowers, and excess heat.

To promote the flowering of the buds, and to avoid stem curvature, remove the top 2 – 3″ (5 – 8 cm) of the stem.

Aquilegia species

Special notes: Aquilegia is very prone to wilting and should not be left out of water for any longer than necessary.

Antirrhinum majus

AQUILEGIA
COLUMBINE, GRANNY'S BONNET

A. caerulea, A. canadensis, A. chrysantha, A. flabellata; and hybrids.

From the buttercup family, these are graceful, nodding, funnel-shaped flowers, with long spurs. The common name derives from the Latin, *columba*, meaning "dove".

Season: Mainly May – July and also October – February.
Available in: Most commonly blue and purple, but also pink, white, and yellow.
Lasting time: These flowers are short lived – on average about 5 days.
Flowers: Each bonnet-shaped flower has five petals and a very distinctive, protruding spur. Choose when the flowers are starting to open.
Stems: Approximately 20″ (50 cm).

ARACHNIS
SPIDER ORCHID, SCORPION ORCHID

A. flos-aëris.

Originating from Malaysia and Indonesia, Arachnis are climbing orchids, on stems several yards long before cutting. The flowers have a faint scent of musk.

Season: All year round.
Available in: Yellow/bronze/reddish-brown, purple spots.
Lasting time: 7 – 10 days.
Flowers: The flowers have long, slender petals which are striped or spotted. Each is about 1½″ (4 cm) across. Select when several flowers are already open.
Stems: Long, thin, and arching. 12 – 24″ (30 – 60 cm).
Special notes: These orchids will last well if they are kept cool and frequently misted. They are very sensitive to ethylene gas and should be kept away from mature fruit and vegetables, dying flowers, and excess heat.

Arachnis flos-aëris

ARANTHERA
SCORPION ORCHID

Aranthera species.

This orchid is a cross between Arachnis and Renanthera, and the most popular hybrid is called "James Storei" which was developed in the Singapore Botanic Gardens in the late 1930s.
Season: All year round.
Available in: Orange-red, bronze.
Lasting time: A fairly long cut life of 10 – 14 days.
Flowers: Each stem bears approximately 8 small, long-petalled blooms, each 1½ – 2" (4 – 6 cm) across. Choose when at least half of the blooms on the spike are fully opened.

Stems: Slender and arching. 12 – 20" (30 – 50 cm).
Special notes: As other orchids, Aranthera are sensitive to ethylene gas and should be kept away from mature fruit and vegetables, dying flowers, and excess heat. Keep them frequently misted.

ASCLEPIAS
MILKWEED, BUTTERFLY WEED, SWALLOW WORT, BLOOD FLOWER

A. tuberosa.

Named after Aesculapius, son of Apollo, and god of healing in Greek mythology.

Season: June – September.

Aranthera species

Asclepias tuberosa

Available in: Bright orange.

Lasting time: Around a week.

Flowers: Round clusters of tiny, crown-like flowers, about ¼" (0.6 cm) wide, form into dense, erect, 2"- (5 cm-) wide umbels. The waxy florets will continue to open throughout the vase life.

Stems: Thick. When cut, usually 12 – 16" (30 – 40 cm).

Special notes: Asclepias are prone to wilting if left out of water for any length of time. Avoid placing in direct sunlight or anywhere too warm.

As new florets open, the old florets will turn brown and die. Remove these as this occurs.

ASTER
MICHAELMAS DAISY, NEW ENGLAND ASTER, NEW YORK ASTER, SEPTEMBER FLOWER

A. cordifolius, A. ericoides, A. novae-angliae, A. novi-belgii; and hybrids.

Asters are a useful intermediary, or filler-flower, in traditional designs both large and small. *A. ericoides* and *A. cordifolius* cultivars, with their particularly small flower heads, are especially popular as a filler for bouquets. From the Latin for star, and the Greek *aster-iskos*, "small star", the clusters of tiny, white, daisy-like flowers of *A. ericoides* (September flower) form on the numerous branches of each stem.

Aster ericoides

Season: *A.ericoides* (September flower) can be found all year round; *A. novi-belgii* between August and October.

Available in: White, pink, and mainly with yellow centers (*A. ericoides*). Lilac, blue, purple, red, and white (*A. novi-belgii*).

Lasting time: 14 – 18 days. Michaelmas daisies are shorter-lasting than September flower – usually just about a week.

Flowers: *A. ericoides* has tiny, daisy-like flowers. If they have been cut too early, the flowers will not open, so buy when the majority are already open on the spray. *A. novi-belgii* have larger flowers, each approximately 1 – 3" (2.5 – 8 cm) across. These should be chosen when most of the flowers on the stem are open.

Aster novi-belgii

Stems: Slender and erect, stalks are borne off a single stem of approximately 12 – 36" (30 – 90 cm).
Special notes: Be sure to remove all leaves below the water level, as these very quickly pollute the vase water in warm conditions.
    Suitable for drying.

ASTILBE
FALSE GOAT'S BEARD, FALSE SPIRAEA

A. arendsii hybrids; *A. chinensis, A. simplicifolia*; and hybrids.

Originating from China, Japan, and Korea, these feathery flowers are now cultivated all over the world. Japonica hybrids (*A. chinensis*) are the dwarf variety, generally having shorter stems than the *A. arendsii* hybrids which flower earlier. These make an attractive alternative to more traditional foliage, and usually come with their own mid- to deep-green leaves. The translation of the word Astilbe from the Greek is "not glittering," a reference to the inconspicuous nature of the individual flowers.

Season: June – September.
Available in: Red, pink, white.
Lasting time: About 7 days, although the leaves will tend to die off before the flowers. Vase life can be improved by sealing the stems (see below).
Flowers: Erect flower plumes of tiny, fluffy flowers. Select when fully developed.
Stems: Slender, erect stems of 15 – 28" (40 – 70 cm). The dwarf varieties are 6 – 8" (15 – 20 cm).
Special notes: Keep in deep water and in a

Astilbe arendsii

Astilbe arendsii

The frilly *Alchemilla mollis* and frothy white *Saponaria* are intertwined with heads of pink *Hydrangea* to made a country garland.

An abundance of *Hydrangea*, *Scabious* and *Saponaria* – overflowing from a country basket – look as if they have just been picked.

cool atmosphere. Vase life can be improved by cutting. Stems will "bleed" when cut, so dip them in boiling water for about 5 seconds.

Suitable for drying.

ASTRANTIA
MASTERWORT

A. major, A. carniolica.

"Alba" is the main white variety, and "Rubra" the red. Astrantia does have a slight musty smell, but it will not be noticed from a distance. It is excellent for use in small delicate designs of mixed flowers.

Season: June – August.
Available in: Green-pink, pink, white, red.
Lasting time: 5 – 10 days.
Flowers: These flower heads, about 1" (2.5 cm) across, resemble pincushions, with many "pins" surrounded by a frill of petals. Choose when most of the flowers on the clustered flower head are open.
Stems: 20 – 24" (50 – 60 cm).
Special notes: Suitable for drying.

Astrantia major

ATRIPLEX
RED MOUNTAIN SPINACH, ORACH

Atriplex species.

A relative of the dock family, this tall crimson-and-green-leaved plant has seed heads appearing along virtually the length of each stem. This is a very popular choice in autumnal arrangements.

Season: All year round.
Available in: Red-brown.
Lasting time: 6 – 10 days.
Flowers: Small seed heads form into several dense spires on each stem.
Stems: 36 – 60" (90 – 150 cm).
Special notes: Suitable for drying.

Atriplex species

Banksia species

BANKSIA
BOTTLEBRUSH, BIRD'S NEST

B. baxteri, B. burdettii, B. coccinea, B. collina,
B. ericifolia, B. occidentalis, B. speciosa; and others.

Named after Sir Joseph Banks (1743 – 1820), who travelled the world collecting plants, including this Protea which originates from Tasmania and Australia. There are several varieties, which vary slightly in shape and color, and it is by shape and size that Banksia are divided. The spiny foliage of these exotic plants makes them a dramatic point in arrangements.

Season: All year round; however the main period is between October and May.

Available in: Red/orange, yellow, and cream.

Lasting time: 14 – 21 days.

Flowers: The flower heads (a dense collection of tiny flowers) stand singly at the end of the stems. These typically cylindrical heads, of about 4 – 10" (10 – 25 cm) in length, are either cup-shaped (*B. baxteri, B. burdetti, B. speciosa, B. victoriae*), or bottle-brush shaped (*B. aus-*

tralis, *B. attenuata, B. coccinea, B. occidentalis*), and they come in various sizes. Select when fully developed, since the flowers do not continue to open once cut.

Stems: Woody stems of 10 – 20" (25 – 50 cm). Cut ends using secateurs.

Special notes: These plants are suitable for drying – in fact they will dry easily simply by being left without water.

BOUVARDIA
BOUVARDIA

B. longiflora; and hybrids.

The genus is named after Charles Bouvard (1571 – 1658), personal physician to King Louis XIII of France and also director of the *Jardin des Plantes*. Originating from Mexico, this flowering shrub is now widely cultivated,

Bouvardia hybrids

Beautiful pink *Nerines*, combined with pink and white *Phlox* and *Lavandula* make a strong, eye-catching display in three colors.

Aster novi-belgii, *Asclepias* and *Agapanthus* combined together make a striking use of color in a loose country-style arrangement.

especially in Holland. *Bouvardia longiflora* is very fragrant, but most Bouvardia hybrids have little or no scent. For drama, mix red Bouvardia with red Anemones and Amaryllis (Hippeastrum).

Season: Primarily April to December, although Dutch cultivation of hybrids means that it is available in most seasons.

Available in: Bright white, cream, pink, red.

Lasting time: 14 – 20 days.

Flowers: Showy, in loose clusters of tubular flowers. Each cluster is approximately 6" (15 cm) wide. Generally these flowers should be bought when the first 2 to 3 florets have started to open; however white varieties, such as "Artemis," should be selected when the buds are showing color, but before they have opened.

Stems: Approximately 20 – 24" (50 – 70 cm). Frequent re-cutting of the stems will help with water absorption, but will not be necessary if the special flower food for Bouvardia is added to the vase water.

Special notes: Bouvardia is particularly prone to water loss and should never be left out of water. Ideally, after purchase, stand Bouvardia for 24 hours in deep, cool water (with flower food added) before arranging. Whenever possible, use the special flower food available (this is often supplied with the cut flower.) To encourage the flowers to last, remove the top bud and excess foliage.

BUPLEURUM
BUPLEURUM

B. griffithii.

Bupleurum is ancient Greek for an umbelliferous plant – meaning that equal-length stalks of individual flowers proceed from a common center, like the spokes of an umbrella. Bupleurum is becoming a popular filler.

Season: All year round.

Available in: Greenish-yellow.

Lasting time: 8 – 14 days.

Flowers: Tiny.

Stems: 18 – 28" (50 – 70 cm).

Bupleurum griffithii

CALENDULA
POT MARIGOLD

C. officinalis; and hybrids.

Officinale means "healing", and the marigold is used in numerous homeopathic remedies and beauty treatments. It probably originates

Calendula officinalis

from southern Europe and has been cultivated since ancient times. The leaves and stems of the plant have a distinctive scent. These are excellent for informal and simple arrangements, and look good in county-style arrangements with dried grasses and foliage.

Season: Most of the year. Peak period April – June.
Available in: Bright orange and shades of yellow.
Lasting time: About a week.
Flowers: Daisy-like, and up to 4" (10 cm) across. There are some double types available, and these may have a contrasting central eye in a red-brown color.
Stems: Shortish stems of 10 – 14" (25 – 35 cm).
Special notes: Edible marigold petals are sometimes available in supermarkets for sprinkling on salads, but commercially-grown marigold are post-harvest-treated and not suitable for eating.

CALLISTEPHUS
CHINA ASTER

C. chinensis hybrids.

The botanical name is derived from the Greek *kalli*, meaning "beauty," and *stephos*, meaning "wreath." This describes the circle of colored petals. China Asters have a very faint scent. The regular, rounded forms of, for example, "Powder puff" are unusual and look especially striking in modern or free-form designs.

Season: July – October.
Available in: Red, pink, blue, yellow, white, cream. Often with contrasting yellow or white centers.
Lasting time: Approximately 7 days, and often longer.

Callistephus chinensis

Flowers: These large flowers come in a variety of shapes – singles, doubles and spider-like. Among the most spectacular examples are "Ostrich plume" (mauve in color) and "Bouquet powder puff," both of which have large double flowers. Select when the flowers are just starting to open.

Stems: 20 – 26" (50 – 66 cm) long, with several large flowers at the top and several smaller ones lower down.

Special notes: In warm conditions, China Asters will quickly pollute the vase water. To help prevent this, remove excess stem foliage before placing in water, and change water regularly, adding fresh flower food when you do so.

CAMPANULA
BELLFLOWER, CANTERBURY BELL,
HAREBELL, CUP AND SAUCER
FLOWER, CHIMNEY BELLFLOWER

C. glomerata, C. persicifolia, C. pyramidalis.

C. persicifolia (Peach-leaved Campanula) was first cultivated in Belgium in 1554, but probably originated from central and southern

Campanula persicifolia

Campanula glomerata

Europe. "Alba" is the popular, white variety. The pastel shades blend well with other summer flowers, especially in massed arrangements – as wedding displays, for example.

C. pyramidalis (Chimney Bellflower), however, was cultivated much later, in 1830, in England, where it is still a popular garden flower.

C. glomerata (Clustered Bellflower) is very different from other varieties; the deep violet-blue flowers forming densely-packed flower heads.

Campanula pyramidales

Season: March – September.
Available in: White, blue, lilac, purple, pink.
Lasting time: Approximately 8 – 15 days.
Flowers: Cup- or bell-shaped flowers – hence the derivation of the name, from the Latin for "bell", *campanula*. Some cultivars have double flowers. *C. pyramidalis* has its flowers borne on long spires.
Stems: Strong, erect, and slender, about 20 – 24" (50 – 60 cm) when cut.

CARTHAMUS
SAFFLOWER

C. tinctorius.

The ancient Egyptians used these bright orange flowers as an effective yellow dye. Carthamus are now cultivated and are very popular in Holland.

Season: June – September.
Available in: Orange-yellow.
Lasting time: 8 – 14 days. Although the flow-

Carthamus tinctorius

ers are fairly long-lasting, the foliage will begin to wilt before the flowers are finished, so they are not ideal for long-term displays.
Flowers: Unusual in shape, numerous thin, orange petals protrude from the spherical green center, which is about 1 inch in diameter. Safflower should only be selected when the majority of buds are clearly opening.
Stems: Short branches extend from a single stem which is between 24" and 30" (60 – 76 cm) when cut.
Special notes: Avoid extremes of temperature.

Especially good for drying.

CATTLEYA
CORSAGE ORCHID

Cattleya hybrids.

These perfectly-shaped orchids were named in 1824 after William Cattley, a wealthy British merchant who collected exotic plants. Originating in Central and South America, Cattleya hybrids are cultivated all over the world, and in particular in the USA. They are grown for bright colors, seasonal flowering and full shape. Often each stem will be placed in an individual water tube, wrapped in wax paper, and placed in a box to protect it in transit from its grower. Some have a slight perfume.

Season: All year round.
Available in: Lavender, white, yellow, pink, orange. The lip of the flower is usually darker than the other petals.
Lasting time: A medium, cut life of 7 – 12 days.
Flowers: The flowers measure between 2¾" and 5" (7 – 12 cm), and typically have a fringed lip. One or more flowers appear at the end of each stem. Choose when they are open.
Stems: 12 – 20" (30 – 50 cm).
Special notes: These flowers are sensitive to ethylene gas and should be kept away from mature fruit and vegetables, dying flowers, and excess heat.

The leaves of Cattleya are sold as Orca foliage.

Cattleya hybrid

Short stems of *Digitalis* blend with the pink-lilac shades of *Godetia*, offset by the dramatic cream and green of *Euonymus* foliage.

CELOSIA
CHINESE WOOL FLOWER, PRINCE OF WALES' FEATHER, COCKSCOMB

C. argentea , (*cristata* and *plumosa* hybrids).

C. argentea plumosa hybrids have large, plume-like flowers, hence their common name, "Prince of Wales' Feather." *C. argentea cristata* hybrids have a broad, comb-shaped inflorescence, and are known as "Cockscomb." Both species come in dwarf and tall varieties.

Season: May – September.
Available in: Scarlet, crimson, yellow (*plumosa*), and red (*cristata*)
Lasting time: 6 – 10 days (*cristata* is longer-lasting than *plumosa*). Remove leaves for good vase life.
Flowers: These flowers have most unusual shapes: *plumosa* is large and plume-like; *cristata* is undulating and comb-shaped. Choose when the flowers are fully mature.
Stems: 24 – 30" (60 – 76 cm).
Special notes: Remove all foliage before arranging.
   Celosia varieties dry quite successfully.

Celosia argentea cristata

CENTAUREA
CORNFLOWER, BACHELOR'S BUTTON, BLUEBOTTLE

C. cyanus.

C. cyanus is usually blue, hence the name cyanus, which is from the Greek *kuaneos*, meaning "dark blue." A wild, cornfield weed, first cultivated in 1480, it is an attractively informal flower and it can look wonderful in a mixed country arrangement with, for example, Agapanthus, Echinops, Eryngium, and Limonium.

Season: May – October.
Available in: Primarily blue, occasionally white or pink.
Lasting time: 5 – 7 days.
Flowers: Thistle-like flowers, approximately 1" (2.5 cm) across.
Stems: Slightly brittle. 16 – 20" (40 – 50 cm).
Special notes: Remove any foliage likely to be submerged in a vase, for it decays very rapidly.
   This is a very popular flower for drying.

Celosia argentea plumosa

Centaurea cyanus

LARGE-HEADED CENTAUREA
....

C. macrocephala.

Centaurea macrocephala is a much larger-headed, thistle-like flower than *Centaurea cyanus*, and has dense foliage. The flower head stands singly at the end of the stem.

Centaurea macrocephala

Season: May – August.
Available: Yellow.
Lasting time: 7 – 14 days.
Flowers: A large, unusually-shaped, thistle-headed flower of approximately 3″ (8 cm) across.
Stems: Thick and approximately 20″ (50 cm) in length.

CHAMAELAUCIUM
WAX FLOWER, TEA-TREE, GERALTON WAX PLANT

C. uncinatum.

Chamaelaucium uncinatum

Originating from western Australia, where it is one of the most popular fillers for bouquets, this aromatic shrub has tiny flowers. Chamaelaucium is often confused with Leptospermum.

Season: October – May, with a peak period between December and February.
Available in: White, lilac-pink, red.
Lasting time: 10 – 14 days.
Flowers: Star-shaped, waxy flowers formed in clusters. Select when the majority of the ½″ (1 cm) wide flowers have begun to open.
Stems: 16 – 20″ (40 – 50 cm).
Special notes: Suitable for drying.

A wide-mouthed vase gives space for the arching stems of *Moluccella* around a dense nucleus of blue *Scabious* and thistly *Eryngium*.

Chrysanthemum indicum (single spray)

CHRYSANTHEMUM

C. carinatum, C. coccineum, C. frutescens, C. maximum, C. morifolium (syn. *indicum*), *C. parthenium*; and hybrids.

The name Chrysanthemum is derived from the Greek, *khrus anthemon, khrusos* meaning "gold," and *anthemon*, "flower." One of the most long-lasting of cut flowers, there are literally hundreds of different varieties of this member of the daisy family, with newly-cultivated introductions every year.

Chrysanthemums are amongst the top five most cultivated and popular flowers.

Chrysanthemum indicum (standard)

Chrysanthemum indicum (anemone-shaped spray)

FLORIST'S CHRYSANTHEMUMS, MUMS
....

C. morifolium and *C. indicum* hybrids.

They can be divided into two main types: "standard" Chrysanthemums and "spray." Standard or single Chrysanthemums are often referred to as "blooms." As the name suggests, these comprise a single flower head – around 4" (10 cm) in diameter – at the end of a single stem. By far the most popular and extensively-cultivated type is the spray Chrysanthemum, also known as a "bunch" Chrysanthemum, where 3 to 7 flower heads appear on branchlets off a single stem.

Within this group there are: single sprays, which resemble daisies; double sprays, where the flowers consist almost entirely of rayed petals, sometimes forming a globe head; "spiders," which have narrow curled petals of irregular lengths; "pompom" or "buttons," which have smaller, tightly-knit flower heads; and anemone-shaped, which have centers of tubular-shaped petals surrounded by one or more rows of rayed petals.

The classification of Chrysanthemums is manifold. Because of the wide diversity in shape and size of bloom, and also of flowering time, they do not fall into succinct categories. However, it will not be difficult to purchase types based on description of flower heads.

Season: All year round.
Available in: Yellow, white, pink, and two-color.

Lasting time: Long lasting, they may well survive over 14 days.

Flowers: Select spray Chrysanthemums when most of the florets have opened, and standard Chrysanthemums when the flower heads are at least half open. If they are bought in green bud, it is possible that they may not open at all.

Stems: 20 – 24″ (50 – 60 cm).

Special notes: Since the foliage usually dies before the blooms, it is advisable to remove all the dead leaves as soon as possible, and re-cut the stems.

Chrysanthemums emit a large amount of ethylene gas, and, unless they are kept in very cool conditions, they are best kept separate from ethylene-sensitive flowers like Dianthus, Antirrhinums, and orchids.

Check water levels regularly.

MARGUERITE, BOSTON DAISY

C. frutescens.

Another daisy-like Chrysanthemum, which grows on a bushy shrub with feathery and almost blue-green leaves. Originally from the Canary Islands, marguerites are also increasing in popularity as a potted plant.

For a simple, pretty arrangement, combine white marguerites with white Narcissi.

Season: May – October.

Available in: White with yellow centers, yellow, pink.

Lasting time: 8 – 14 days.

Flowers: 1¼ – 2¾″ (3 – 7 cm) across, consisting of a yellow center surrounded by white, yellow, or pink petals. Choose when most of the

Chrysanthemum frutescens

Chrysanthemum parthenium (button)

Chrysanthemum parthenium (standard)

flowers have already opened.
Stems: 10 – 16" (25 – 40 cm).
Special notes: The flowers are sometimes tinted with dyes.

FEVERFEW, MATRICARIA, CAPENSIS

C. parthenium.

Daisy-like, this flower has pungently aromatic leaves.

Season: April – December.

Available in: White, cream, yellow
Lasting time: 7 – 14 days.
Flowers: Small with white petals and yellow centers, or button shaped. Select as the flowers are starting to open.
Stems: Long stems of 20 – 28" (50 – 70 cm).
Special notes: The leaves and flowers have a pungent, spicy scent similar to camomile.

SHASTA DAISY

C. maximum hybrids.

A large daisy flower, where the petals are a little irregular, giving a slightly shaggy appearance. The most frequently cultivated variety is the double-flowered "Wirral Supreme," where the flower has pointed petals and an unkempt appearance. These Chrysanthemums are often tinted with green, blue, pink, and yellow dyes. They have an informality about them and look marvellous either used generously in a massed arrangement or in small numbers mixed in a foliage arrangement.

Season: May – July.
Available in: White petals with a golden eye. Occasionally tinted.
Lasting Time: 7 – 14 days.
Flowers: These are single flowers of 2½ – 3" (6 – 8 cm) across. Double forms are a little larger. Choose when flowers are fully open.
Stems: These are strong, and approximately 16" (40 cm) high.

Chrysanthemum maximum

Rosa and *Ananas* – a striking contrast, but one that nevertheless shows that roses really are the perfect flower and combine with just about anything.

Convallaria majalis

CIRSIUM
CNICUS, PLUMED THISTLE

C. japonicum, C. rivulare.

The name Cirsium is derived from the old Greek word *kirsion*, meaning "thistle", and this flower was reputed to cure varicose veins. The leaves and stems are covered with masses of fine prickles.

Cirsium japonicum

Season: All year round.
Available in: Red, purple, and pale pink.
Lasting time: 5 – 7 days.
Flowers: Small, thistle-like flowers, approximately ¾ – 1¼" (2 – 3 cm) across, appear in clusters at the end of the stems. Choose when the flowers are open.
Stems: Stems range from 24 – 36" (60 – 90 cm).
Special notes: Suitable for drying.

CONVALLARIA
LILY OF THE VALLEY

C. majalis and cultivars.

These small, bell-shaped flowers, which appear on pale-green stems, carry a sweet and memorable perfume. Lily of the valley are often incorporated into bridal headdresses and bouquets. If used as an arrangement, they look best displayed simply. They are available in single and double forms, but the most commonly found are the single, white form.

In addition, Convallaria foliage, in green and in variegated-yellow, is excellent in designs. It is stiff and upright. The small reddish berries that form in the fall are also used in arrangements.

Season: May is the main time of year for these flowers, but there is limited availability for the rest of the year.
Available in: White, and occasionally pink.
Lasting time: 4 – 6 days.
Flowers: Bell-shaped, waxy flowers, about ¼" (6 mm) long, are borne in several clusters. These are often surrounded by several broad, smooth, pointed leaves. Select when flowers are well developed.
Stems: Single, 6 – 8" (15 – 20 cm), arching stems.
Special notes: Lily of the valley are prone to wilting if they are exposed to heat or are left without water for prolonged lengths of time.
Suitable for drying.

COREOPSIS
TICKSEED

C. grandiflora, C. lanceolata, C. tinctoria, C, verticillata; and hybrids.

Sometimes called Calliopsis, these daisy-like, summer flowers originate from central and eastern USA. These look good in very small arrangements. Some double hybrids exist.

Season: June – August.
Available in: Yellow, sometimes with an orange/brown center.
Lasting time: Approximately 7 days.
Flowers: Daisy-like flowers, of about 1 – 2" (2.5 – 5 cm) across, which should be selected when the flowers are fully developed.
Stems: 16 – 20" (40 – 50 cm).

COSMEA
COSMOS

C. bipinnatus, C. sulphureus; and hybrids.

This very bright, showy, summer flower has been cultivated in Europe since the eighteenth century, and is now grown outdoors in all the major flower-growing countries of the world.

The size of *C. bipinnatus* flower heads makes them useful for larger arrangements. The smaller blooms of *C. sulphureus* are useful for sprinkling throughout a smaller-scale arrangement, or making up a miniature design.

Season: July – September.
Available in: Bright pink, red, white, lavender, orange, yellow.

Coreopsis grandiflora

Coreopsis grandiflora (double flowered)

Cosmea sulphureus

Lasting time: Approximately 4 – 9 days.
Flowers: This flower has heads up to 4" (10 cm) across, with a flat face. *C. bipinnatus* hybrids have daisy-like flowers with contrasting center colors and ferny foliage. *C. sulphureus* hybrids are smaller. Choose when the petals have opened but are not yet lying flat.
Stems: *C. bipinnatus* hybrids have tall stems of 16 – 30" (40 – 76 cm); and *C. sulphureus*, approximately 6 – 8" (15 – 20 cm).
Special notes: The life of this relatively short-lived flower is prolonged if it is kept away from draughts, heat, and direct sunshine.

CRASPEDIA
DRUMSTICK

C. glauca, C. globosa.

Originating from New Zealand, this tight ball of tiny flowers occurs at the end of a straight, leafless stem.

Season: May – October.
Available in: Yellow.

Lasting time: 12 – 15 days.
Flowers: Hard, globular flower heads.
Stems: 12 – 18" (30 – 40 cm).
Special notes: Suitable for drying.

Craspedia glauca

CROCOSMIA
MONTBRETIA

C. pottsii.

Crocosmia is from the Iris family, and is related to Gladioli. The name is derived from the Greek *krokos*, meaning "saffron" – a reference to the bright orange of the most cultivated variety. Although unscented, Crocosmia are excellent as cut flowers, and their sword-like foliage is extremely useful for arrangers.

Season: June – September.
Available in: Yellow, orange, red.
Lasting time: A medium-length cut life of 7 – 10 days.
Flowers: Double ranks of 1½"- (4 cm-) long, trumpet-shaped flowers open from the bottom

Crocosmia pottsii

of the spike upwards, over a period of about a week, and are borne in graceful, arching panicles. Choose when buds have started to show color but have not yet opened.

Stems: Wiry, arching stems about 15 – 25" (38 – 63 cm) high.

Special notes: Crocosmia are particularly sensitive to ethylene gas and should be kept away from mature fruit and vegetables, dying flowers, and excess heat.

Remove lower florets as they die.

CYMBIDIUM
CYMBIDIUM ORCHID

Cymbidium hybrids.

The ancestors of these exotic orchids came from Asia and Australia, and they are now cultivated all over the world. They are usually available in single stems or branches, which bear 8 to 12 flowers, but miniature hybrids can produce up to 25 flowers per stem. Cymbidium have become a very popular and typical flower for corsages, but can also look wonderful displayed together as long stems in different color varieties.

Cymbidium hybrid (miniature)

Season: All year round, with a peak period between October and December.
Available in: Red-orange, pink, yellow-green, white.
Lasting time: Long-lasting. At least 14 days.
Flowers: These may be erect or pendulous. The average stem bears around 12 flowers on a spike, each 3 – 4" (7 – 10 cm) across. Miniature varieties are approximately 2" (5 cm) across, and there may be as many as 20 flowers on a spray. Select when all of the lower blooms are opening.
Stems: Sturdy stems of 20 – 24" (50 – 60 cm). Miniature varieties may be about 5" (13 cm) shorter.
Special notes: Cymbidium require a cool and moist atmosphere. Frequent fresh water and flower food, as well as misting, will ensure longevity. Avoid excess heat or draughts.

DAHLIA
DAHLIA

Dahlia hybrids.

Dahlia hybrid (double flowered)

Named after the Swedish botanist Anders Dahl (1751 – 1789), this bright flower originates from Mexico and has been extensively cultivated in Europe since the nineteenth century. Dahlias come in many different shapes and sizes, and for ease of reference these can be divided into:

SINGLE-FLOWERED types, where there is a single row of petals (including the Collerette form with an additional "collar" of shorter petals).

A range of DOUBLE-FLOWERED types, where there are double rows of petals – such as Anemone, and Peony-flowering – and including the fully double Decorative Dahlias, where the central disc is completely obscured, and Ball or pompom Dahlias where the petals form a globe.

Cymbidium hybrid (standard)

Heavily scented *longiflorum* and oriental-hybrid "Stargazer" *Lilium* need their pollen-laden stamens snipped off if they are placed near precious furnishings.

CACTUS types, where the flowers are semi-double and the florets are pointed.

The striking shape of the Cactus Dahlia adds impact to a bold, free-form or modern design. The Decorative Dahlias, however, having more rounded petals, lend themselves to more sophisticated, traditional-style arrangements.

Season: July – October.
Available in: Red, orange, pink, yellow, white, lavender; including two-color cultivars.
Lasting time: On average about 6 days, but the life of Dahlias will be extended by lightly spraying with water.
Flowers: Closely-petalled and showy. In general the blooms range from about 4 – 6" (10 – 15 cm) across, although Decorative, Ball, and Cactus types can be as large as 10" (25 cm). Select when flowers are starting to open.
Stems: 10 – 24" (25 – 60 cm).
Special notes: Suitable for drying, especially the pompom varieties.

It is recommended that foliage is removed.

Dahlias are thirsty flowers, so check water levels regularly.

Dahlia hybrid (pompom)

Dahlia hybrid (collarette, single flowered)

DELPHINIUM
DELPHINIUM

Delphinium hybrids (usually of *D. elatum*).

Named from the Latin *delphis* meaning "dolphin," Delphinium have been cultivated in the countries around the Mediterranean since ancient times. The original flowers were blue, but recent cultivars are pink, lilac, and white.

The ancestors of these elegant flowers came mainly from China, but now new cultivars are being bred all over the world. Their flowering period coincides with Campanula which, with its similar colorings but contrasting form, makes a good combination.

Season: All year round, but with a main season between May and September.
Available in: Blue, purple, salmon pink, white.
Lasting time: 10 – 12 days.
Flowers: The stately, showy 8 – 10" (20 – 25 cm)

Delphinium elatum

spires of open flowers, each about ½" (1 cm) across, are heavy and need careful handling. Choose when most of the lower flowers on the spike have opened.

Stems: Soft stemmed. Extremely tall, ranging from 28 – 72" (70 – 180 cm). However, the popular hybrids of *D. elatum* are between 15" and 30" (38 – 76 cm).

Special notes: The plant is poisonous.

Delphinium are ethylene-gas sensitive and should be kept away from mature fruit and vegetables, dying flowers, and excess heat. In warm conditions, therefore, the water may need to be changed every few days, and flower food added.

These are very good for air-drying. They need about 3 – 4 weeks in a light, warm atmosphere.

The foliage is best removed to prevent polluting vase water.

LARKSPUR

....

D. consolida.

These Delphinium hybrids look beautiful in mixed designs. They have more delicate foliage than standard Delphiniums.

Season: All year round, but with a peak period from June – September.

Available in: Shades of blue, pink, lilac, and white.

Lasting time: A medium, cut life of about 10 days.

Flowers: Numerous flowers, of about ½ – 1" (1 – 2.5 cm) across, are closely packed on each stem.

Stems: Stem length can range from small, 12 – 24" (30 – 61 cm), to tall types, 48 – 60" (121 – 152 cm), that look like standard Delphiniums.

Special notes: This plant is poisonous.

Larkspur are amongst the most commonly available of the ready-dried flowers to be found at florists.

Delphinium consolida

DENDROBIUM
DENDROBIUM ORCHID, SINGAPORE ORCHIDS, POMPADOUR

D. phalaenopsis; and hybrids.

The largest genera of orchid, in which there is considerable diversity of form. The numerous hybrids are exported mainly from Thailand,

Lime-green *Moluccella* and green-and-white striped *Euphorbia marginata* are mixed with the clover-like flower heads of *Gomphrena* for an effective abundance of foliage and dry-textured flowers.

Singapore, and Hawaii. Mix red Dendrobium with red roses for a stunning bouquet.

Season: All year round

Available in: White, purple, yellow-green, pink, red. Some varieties are dyed, others have curled or striped petals.

Lasting time: Quite a long cut life of around 14 – 21 days.

Flowers: Despite the diversity of form, the flowers of this genera all have the same structure. The small flowers of *D. phalaenopsis* are about 1" (2.5 cm) across, and about 10 to 12 flowers will be found per stem. The most popular cut-flower cultivars are "Madame Pompadour" in dark pink and "Madame Pompadour Wit" in white.

Stems: 12 – 20" (30 – 50 cm).

Special notes: Dendrobium require a cool and moist atmosphere. Frequent misting with water will ensure longevity. Avoid excess heat or draughts.

All orchids are sensitive to ethylene gas and should be kept away from mature fruit and vegetables, dying flowers, and excess heat.

Dendrobium phalaenopsis

DIANTHUS
CARNATIONS, SPRAY CARNATIONS

D. caryophyllus hybrids.

Dianthus have been famous since classical times for their beauty, and in Greek, *dianthus* means "divine flower." The common name, however, is a corruption of the word "coronation."

The *caryophyllus* hybrids are amongst the top five most cultivated and popular flowers in the world, and are available in a vast array of colors. Their fragrance ranges from very slight to pronounced.

In general, carnations are graded according to stem length and flower size and, in the case of spray carnations, by the number of heads per stem. The highest grades have longer stems and larger flower heads. The simplest division is between single-flower heads and spray carnations.

Season: All year round.

Available in: A huge color range – naturally occurring in virtually every color except blue. Can be found in two and three tones. Sometimes florists will even dye carnations to get hues of green and blue.

Lasting time: 7 – 21 days.

Flowers: The single-head carnations have flowers 2 – 3" (5 – 8 cm) in diameter, whereas the spray carnations have 3 – 7 flowers per stem and are 1¼ – 1½" (3 – 4 cm) in diameter.

Select when the majority of the buds are showing color and some flowers are already open.

Stems: 16 – 28" (40 – 70 cm). The highest quality of carnation, called "select," has long, 28 – 36" (71 – 91 cm) stems, and flowers up to 3½" (9 cm) in diameter. Mini types have 12 – 30" (30 – 76 cm).

Special notes: All Dianthus are sensitive to ethylene gas and should be kept away from mature fruit and vegetables, dying flowers, and excess heat.

Cut the stem between the stem nodes to aid water absorption.

Spray carnations are suitable for drying.

Dianthus caryophyllus (spray)

Dianthus caryophyllus (single headed)

SWEET WILLIAM

....

D. barbatus.

A popular garden flower, *D. barbatus* is commercially grown from spring to early fall. Of the many varieties, "Scarlet Beauty" (red), "Pink Beauty" (clear pink), "Diadem" (red with a white center), and "Crimson" (dark copper red) are widely available.

Dianthus barbatus

Season: May – October, with a peak period May – June.
Available in: White, pink, red, two-color.
Lasting time: 7 – 10 days.
Flowers: Many small flowers form into dense, flattish heads approximately 3 – 5" (8 – 13 cm) in diameter. Select when the flowers are starting to open.
Stems: 20 – 28" (50 – 70 cm). Buy flowers with straight stems.
Special notes: In warm conditions, vase water may need changing, and the use of flower food is essential. Dianthus are sensitive to ethylene gas and should be kept away from mature fruit and vegetables, dying flowers, and excess heat.

Suitable for drying.

PINKS, BORDER PINK, GARDEN PINK, CHINESE PINK

....

D. plumarius.

Dianthus plumarius

Originating from the mountainous meadows of central Europe, the garden pink was first cultivated in Belgium in 1565 and is now grown all over Europe. Most Dianthus have little scent, but these flowers have a very aromatic and slightly pungent perfume.

Season: All year round, but with a main season May – August.
Available in: White, pink, red.
Lasting time: 8 – 12 days.
Flowers: Only about 3 or 4 buds on each stem will open. Each flower is about 1″ (2.5 cm) across. Select when the few opening buds are starting to show color.
Stems: 12 – 20″ (30 – 50 cm).
Special notes: Dianthus are very sensitive to ethylene gas, so they should be kept away from mature fruit and vegetables, dying flowers, and excess heat.

Suitable for drying.

DIGITALIS
FOXGLOVE

D. ferruginea, D. grandiflora, D. lanata, D. purpurea, D. thapsi; and hybrids.

An indigenous European flower, first cultivated in Switzerland in 1830. The plant is still used to produce a drug for heart complaints. *D. purpurea* is the commonest species.

Digitalis purpurea

Season: Main season April – June.
Available in: Mainly pink and blue, but also red, white, yellow, maroon.
Lasting time: 7 – 10 days.
Flowers: Tightly clustered, large, 2″- (5 cm-) long, bell-shaped, hooded flowers on 12 – 36″ (30 – 91 cm) spikes. Most species have the characteristic, contrasting dark spots inside the bell. Choose when the lower florets are starting to open. Remove wilted lower florets as upper ones open.
Stems: 28 – 36″ (70 – 90 cm). These will block easily and should be regularly re-cut.
Special notes: Digitalis are sensitive to ethylene gas and should be kept away from maturing fruit and vegetables, dying flowers and excess heat.

This plant is poisonous.

Dimorphotheca aurantiaca

DIMORPHOTHECA
CAPE MARIGOLD, AFRICAN DAISY,
STAR OF THE VELDT

D. aurantiaca.

A summer daisy, with a dark center, surrounded by a single circle of petals.

Season: June – September.
Available in: Orange, with a darker center. Also in yellow, white, cream, and pink.

Lasting time: 4 – 6 days.
Flowers: Daisy-like and about 2" (5 cm) in diameter. Select when the flowers are open.
Stems: 12 – 16" (30 – 40 cm).

DORONICUM
LEOPARD'S BANE

D. grandiflorum, D. orientale; and species.

Doronicum species

A European daisy, cultivated since 1808, Doronicum is grown outdoors in temperate areas. The leaves are heart-shaped and the single row of petals surrounds a yellow center.

Season: April – June.
Available in: Yellow.
Lasting time: Short-lived, just 3 – 5 days.
Flowers: Daisy-like and about 2" (5 cm) in diameter. Choose when the flowers are open.
Stems: 12 – 20" (30 – 50 cm).

ECHINOPS
GLOBE THISTLE

E. bannaticus, E. exaltatus, E. humilis, E. ritro.

Echinops means sea urchin, and it is a very accurate description of this tight, prickly flower. Two frequently-cultivated varieties are

Echinops banaticus

"Taplow Blue" (deep blue) and "Veitch Blue" (deep, dark blue). Fresh flowers have a slight scent.

Season: July – September.
Available in: Shades of blue.
Lasting time: 10 – 21 days.
Flowers: Single, spherical heads. Select when blooms are open.
Stems: Stiff, erect, branching stems, of approximately 20 – 30" (50 – 76 cm), bear much divided, thistled foliage.
Special notes: Remove any foliage that is likely to be submerged in vase water.

Suitable for drying and winter displays, Echinops is one of the most commonly available of the ready-dried flowers to be found at florists. When purchased already dried, the flower heads are often dyed a very deep blue.

EREMURUS
FOXTAIL LILY, DESERT CANDLE

E. robustus, E. stenophyllus; and hybrids.

Originating from Iran, Afghanistan, and Turkey, these tall, erect lilies were first cultivated in Britain in 1875. Hybrids have since been produced, particularly in Holland. Because of their height, they are used in expansive or dramatic summer designs of flowers and foliage, and are particularly useful in church arrangements.

Season: June – July.
Available in: Mainly yellow, also white, cream, orange, pink.
Lasting time: About 10 days.
Flowers: Tall, majestic spikes of tiny, densely-packed, star-shaped flowers. The flowers open from the bottom, and will continue to open when standing in water. Select when about a quarter of the lower florets are open.
Stems: Approximately 24 – 36″ (61 – 91 cm), stiff stems. Frequent re-cutting of the stems may help to ensure that the upper florets will open
Special notes: Regular re-cutting of the stems is advisable.

Remove wilted, lower florets as new florets open.

Eremurus species

Erigeron speciosus

ERIGERON
FLEABANE

E. speciosus hybrids.

A small daisy, which has sprays of rather shaggy flower heads. Originating from the USA, it is now cultivated outdoors in temperate areas.

Season: May – August.
Available in: Mainly purple, with a yellow or brown center, but sometimes pink, maroon, or white varieties.
Lasting time: 6 – 10 days.
Flowers: Daisy-like, with numerous florets around a central eye. Each flower head is about 2″ (5 cm) in diameter. Choose when they are just opening.
Stems: 20 – 24″ (50 – 60 cm).
Special notes: Avoid excess heat and draughts so that petals do not dry up.

Re-cut stems frequently.

White *Scabious*, *Hypericum* and *Nigella* make an unusually dramatic statement in a plain vase, when carefully lit.

ERYNGIUM
SEA HOLLY

E. maritimum (syn. E. planum).

Eryngium comes from the old Greek *erungion* from *eruggos*, meaning sea holly. The plant reputedly had a healing effect in cases of colic. The flower heads and their surrounding prickly leaves are bright blue. These thistles originate from central and southern Europe and Siberia. Eryngium is cultivated outdoors during the summer months. Dried, Eryngium makes a particularly attractive winter decoration.

Season: July – September.
Available in: Blue.
Lasting time: Long lasting, approximately 12 – 16 days.

Eryngium planum

Flowers: Small, cone-shaped heads, ¾ – 1" (2 – 2.5 cm) long, of metallic-blue flowers, with a frill of feathery, but sharp, bracts behind it.
Stems: On average, 20 – 28" (50 – 70 cm) in length.
Special notes: The foliage will probably die before the flowers.
    These are very suitable for drying.

ALPINE THISTLE

E. alpinium, E. giganteum.

These thistles have much larger heads and are best used as a free-form display, because they are so dramatic.

Season: July – September.
Available in: Blue.
Lasting time: 12 – 16 days.
Flowers: Steely-blue flower heads, about 1" (2.5 cm) long, are surrounded by large, prominent, spiky bracts of the same color.
Stems: 20 – 28" (50 – 70 cm). Interestingly, the more mature the stems, the less they seem to need to drink.
Special notes: Suitable for drying.

Eryngium alpinium

EUCHARIS
AMAZON LILY, EUCHARIS LILY

E. grandiflora, E.amazonica.

A tropical lily, originating from Colombia and cultivated in Europe since 1853, Eucharis has a soft, but pleasant, scent.

Eucharis grandiflora

Season: All year round, with a peak period in summer.
Available in: White.
Lasting time: Approximately 7 – 10 days.
Flowers: Typically, there are 1 – 4 daffodil-shaped flowers borne at the end of each stem. Each is approximately 2″ (5 cm) in diameter. Choose when they are beginning to open.
Stems: 16 – 20″ (40 – 50 cm).
Special notes: Eucharis lilies need high humidity to ensure longevity, so gently spraying with water will help their vase life.

They should be very carefully handled to avoid bruising their petals.

EUPHORBIA
SCARLET PLUME, FLOWERING SPURGE

E. fulgens.

The *Euphorbia fulgens* shrub originates from Mexico, and is part of the family which includes the familiar poinsettia (*E. pulcherrima*).

Season: October – December.
Available in: Primarily in orange or red, but also in salmon pink, cream, white, yellow.
Lasting time: 6 – 8 days.

Flowers: At about ½″ (1 cm) wide, the small, star-shaped flowers of *E. fulgens* run along the stem in wands. The flowers grow all along the stem.
Stems: The thin branches of the stems, 24 – 39″ (60 – 100 cm), droop naturally into a wide curve.
Special notes: All species exude a sap when cut. Re-cutting the stems under water will cause the sticky sap to coagulate; alternatively dip in boiling water for five seconds.

Leaves tend to drop naturally and do not indicate poor care.

Euphorbia fulgens

SNOW-ON-THE-MOUNTAIN, KENYAN EUPHORBIA, SPURGE

E. marginata.

Euphorbus was a Greek physician in the 1st-century-AD. Unless closely inspected, *E. marginata* looks like foliage without flowers, but it actually has tiny, white flowers in clusters, which appear at the end of each stem. The interesting flower bracts create an unusual sculptural effect in arrangements, and look good in all foliage designs.

Season: All year round, but especially November – February.

A summer collection of *Dianthus barbatus*, *Triteleia*, *Lathyrus* and *Campanula persicifolia*, shown as if they had been picked straight from the garden.

A combination of the dry-textured flowers *Astilbe* and *Limonium*, creates a longer-lasting display.

Euphorbia marginata

Euphorbia polychroma

Available in: White/green.
Lasting time: 7 – 12 days.
Flowers: Small, insignificant flowers are surrounded by conspicuous, green bracts with a petal-like appearance.
Stems: 20 – 30″ (50 – 76 cm) long.
Special notes: A cool atmosphere will encourage longevity.

Euphorbias all contain a white, milky sap, which is highly irritant to sensitive skins. To prevent contact, it is advisable to seal the cut stems in boiling water for 5 seconds.

EUSTOMA
LISIANTHUS, PRAIRIE GENTIAN

E. grandiflora (syn. *Lisianthus russellianthus*).

One of the Gentian family, and native to Japan, North America, and northern Mexico. Eustoma's large, papery petals are really quite hardy, considering their fragile appearance. The newer hybrids have strong color and an extended vase life.

Season: May – October.
Available in: Purple, pink, white, and two-color.
Lasting time: 7 – 20 days.
Flowers: Choose when several of these cupped, anemone-like flowers are open.
Stems: Graceful stems of up to 32″ (80 cm), with many branchlets.

Special notes: Removing wilted flowers will encourage upper buds to open, and improve longevity. Eustoma should be kept away from excess heat, and stems should be re-cut frequently.

Eustoma grandiflora

The long, spiraling heads of *Lysimachia* and pink *Antirrhinum* surround spherical clusters of the black-eyed *Ornithogalum arabicum*.

FREESIA
FREESIA

Freesia hybrids.

Named after F. H. T. Freese (d. 1876), a German physician, the Freesia is a universally popular flower because of its sweet fragrance. The pink and red varieties tend to have a stronger perfume than the other colors.

Freesias are amongst the top five most culti-vated flowers. Combine white Freesias with other white flowers, such as Syringa and *Euphorbia fulgens*, and offset with green foliage.

Freesia hybrids

Season: All year round.
Available in: Most colors. Purple, pink, red, orange, white, yellow, and two-color.
Lasting time: 5 – 7 days.
Flowers: Branched spikes of about six, funnel-shaped blooms, 1½" (4 cm) long. The upper buds will continue to open if the lower and faded flowers are snipped off. As Freesia have a relatively short vase life, it is important to choose blooms with at least one flower open and three to four showing good color.
Stems: Thin. 12 – 24" (30 – 60 cm).
Special notes: Freesias are sensitive to ethylene

gas, so avoid placing them near mature fruit and vegetables, dying flowers, or excess heat. They should never be left without water.
 Suitable for drying.

Galanthus nivalis

GALANTHUS
SNOWDROP

G. nivalis.

The translation of *galanthus* is, roughly, "milk flower," and *nivalis* means "snow white" – indicative of the flower's season and color. As these flowers are so short-lived in a vase, they are more popular as a potted plant.

Season: December – February.
Available in: White.
Lasting time: Approximately 4 days, but a little longer if kept cool.
Flowers: Drooping, white, bell-shaped flowers about 1" (2.5 cm) long, hang from the end of the stems. Select in bud.
Stems: Short. 6 – 8" (15 – 20 cm).
Special notes: The flowers are very fragile and require careful handling.

GARDENIA
CAPE JASMINE

G. jasminoides cultivars.

Taking its name from the American botanist Dr. Alexander Garden (1730 – 1791), this small, evergreen, flowering shrub, with shiny, leathery leaves, bears the most fragrant and delicate of flowers. As their cut life is very short, they should be purchased when the inner petals are still almost closed. They are beautiful for button holes and for use as corsages.

Gardenia jasminoides

Season: Limited supply all the year round, but primarily a summer flower from June to September.
Available in: Creamy-white.
Lasting time: 2 – 3 days.
Flowers: These waxy, double blooms are approximately 3″ (8 cm) across. Select as the outer petals are opening but the inner are still closed.
Stems: 1¼ – 2¾″ (3 – 7 cm). Longer stems are sometimes available, but it is possibly more economical to buy Gardenia as a potted plant and cut stems as required.
Special notes: The flowers need to be kept very cool and misted regularly. The petals bruise and turn brown extremely easily, and should be handled with great care.

GENISTA
BROOM, WARMINSTER BROOM, CANARY ISLAND BROOM, FLORIST'S GENISTA

G. fragrans (syn. *Cytisus* x *spachianus*).

Genista is also referred to as Cytisus, and *Cytisus* x *spachianus* is very similar to C. *canariensis* – often sold as Genista. The small flowers, which cover the upper part of the leafless branches of this shrub, resemble the sweet pea, to which they are related. The flowers have a faint, pleasant fragrance.

The better-quality Genista branches are the terminal ones, while those further back are woodier. Genista can look superb if used sparingly in an arrangement with, say, tulips.

Season: February – April.
Available in: Creamy-white, yellow. It is also often dyed pink, red, or lilac.
Lasting time: 6 – 8 days.
Flowers: A profusion of small, ½″- (1 cm-) long, pea-shaped flowers are closely packed on the stem.
Stems: Wiry, green, leafless branches of 16 – 20″ (40 – 50 cm) in length.
Special notes: Genista is sensitive to ethylene gas and should be kept away from mature fruit and vegetables, dying flowers, and excess heat.

Genista fragrans

Gentiana makinoi

GENTIANA
GENTIAN

G. makinoi hybrids.

Thought to be named after the 2nd-century-BC, Illyrian King, Gentius, who was reputedly the first to use this plant medicinally. The 'makinoi" cultivar originates from Japan and is now mainly grown in Europe.

Season: July – September.
Available in: Blue, white.
Lasting time: 21 – 28 days.
Flowers: Trumpet-shaped.
Stems: 16 – 20" (40 – 50 cm).

GERBERA
TRANSVAAL DAISY, BARBERTON DAISY

G. jamesonii hybrids, *G. viridifolia* hybrids.

The ancestors of these bright and extensively-cultivated daisies were native to South Africa – mainly the Transvaal and Cape Province. An extremely popular and widely-available flower, most of their current cultivation is in Holland, where new varieties are being produced every year, including the popular, mini-sized Gerbera. The newer cultivars have stronger stems than previously, making them less inclined to droop.

Season: All year round. Peak period March – May.
Available in: Most colors. White, pink, red, yellow, orange, and purple; typically with a yellow center.
Lasting time: 5 – 10 days.
Flowers: Large, daisy-like flowers, in single and double forms, of between 2" (5 cm) and 5" (13 cm) across. Select when they are well developed.

Gerbera jamesonii (miniature)

Gerbera jamesonii

Stems: Thin and leafless stems of 10 – 39" (25 – 100 cm). If the stems go limp, cut off 2" (5 cm) and place the flowers in water up to their necks until they become rigid and straight again.

Special notes: Gerbera's longevity can be reduced if there is bacteria in the vase water. Ensure, therefore, that water is fresh and clean, and always add flower food. Keep out of excess heat and direct sunlight.

GLADIOLUS
GLADIOLI, SWORD LILY

Gladiolus hybrids; *G* x *nanus, G* x *colvillei.*

A wide variety of colors have been cultivated from this flower, which originated in Africa. Gladius means "sword" in Latin, and refers to the shape of the leaves. *G.* x *nanus* and *G* x *colvillei* are examples of miniature versions.

These smaller gladioli are gaining popularity as they are suitable for bouquets. Commonly cultivated varieties are "Nymph" (white with a red-edged cream spot), "Spitfire" (red), and "Charm" (salmon pink).

Season: Most of the year. Peak period June – August. The peak period for miniature gladioli is April – July.

Available in: Most colors except blue: e.g. lavender, red, pink, orange, white, yellow. Miniature varieties are available in pink, white, yellow, cream, red, and two-color.

Lasting time: 10 – 16 days. The large- and medium-flowered varieties have a longer cut life than the small and miniature gladioli.

Flowers: Spikes of at least 10 funnel-shaped, brightly-colored flowers, varying in size. When selecting, ensure the buds all show color. The larger-flowered types generally last longer than the smaller varieties.

Stems: Stiff and erect, 30 – 38" (75 – 96 cm). Miniature gladioli stems are 10 – 14" (25 – 35 cm).

Gladiolus hybrids (miniature)

Gladiolus species

Special notes: Removing the lower flowers as they fade encourages upper buds to open. Snipping off the very top couple of buds has the same effect, and will help prevent the stems from curving.

Adding flower food to the water will encourage the flowers to open.

GLORIOSA
GLORY LILY, GLORIOSA LILY

G. rothschildiana, G. superba.

This splendid, exotic lily from tropical Africa is named after Baron Z. W. de Rothschild, who entered the Gloriosa species at an exhibition of the English Royal Horticultural Society

at the turn of the century. Since then it has been cultivated primarily in Holland.

Gloriosa can look marvellous arranged around a plain lily flower. Gloriosa is in fact a vine, and is available as individual flowers in water tubes, or as a whole top vine with several clusters of flowers.

Season: April – October.
Available in: Red, with a yellow stripe; or yellow with orange edges.
Lasting time: 5 – 10 days.
Flowers: A succession of flowers which resemble those of Turk's-cap lilies – having six, narrow petals, curved at their edges. Each flower is about 3 – 4" (8 – 10 cm) across. Choose when flowers are fully ripe.
Stems: Short varieties, 6 – 8" (15 – 20 cm) long, and taller varieties, 14 – 24" (35 – 60 cm) long.
Special notes: These flowers require careful

Gloriosa rothschildiana

Spray *Chrysanthemum* in mixed vibrant shades of pink and cerise contrast with lime green *Moluccella* and the shiny red berries of *Hypericum*.

The cloudy fronds of *Ammi* provide a background for the heavier bells of *Scilla*, making a very fresh color combination of white and blue.

handling to avoid damaging them, and this is why they are often sold in inflated bags.

Wilting flowers can be revived by immersion in deep water for several hours. Regular spraying will help vase life.

Godetia grandiflora

GODETIA
FAREWELL TO SPRING, SATIN FLOWER, CLARKIA

G. grandiflora; and hybrids.

A Californian flower, cultivated in Europe since 1870, and named after the Swiss botanical author C. H. Godet. It is cultivated outdoors in temperate areas. Single and double varieties are available as cut flowers and, interestingly, they will close up in the dark. Godetia is synonymous with Clarkia.

Season: June – September.
Available in: Shades of orange, red, violet, and pink.
Lasting time: 7 – 10 days.
Flowers: Many brightly-colored, funnel-shaped, single or double flowers grow together on each spike. Choose when several flowers are open.
Stems: 12 – 20″ (30 – 50 cm). It is advisable to cut stems under water.
Special notes: Lukewarm water and light will encourage the buds to open, and the lower ones will do so over a period of days. These flowers will take in a lot of water, so check vase level regularly.

GOMPHRENA
GLOBE AMARANTH

G. globosa, G. hageana hybrids.

The name Gomphrena is a corruption of Gomphaena – another plant, the leaves of which were once used medicinally. Resembling the flower heads of clover, Gomphrena are typically used in dried arrangements; they also look superb offsetting a fresh arrangement.

Gomphrena globosa

Season: May – September.
Available in: White, pink, red, purple, and orange.
Lasting time: 7 – 12 days.
Flowers: Colorful, everlasting, clover-like flower heads of only about 1" (2.5 cm) across.
Stems: Approximately 14 – 20" (30 – 50 cm).
Special notes: The flower heads can be successfully dried for winter decoration. The lower flowers may fade before the top blooms, and can be removed when this occurs, or cut initially and used separately.

GYPSOPHILA
GYP, BABY'S BREATH, MAIDEN'S BREATH, CHALK PLANT

G. elegans, G. paniculata.

From the Greek *gupsos*, "chalk," and *philos*, "loving," Gypsophila was originally found on the chalky soils of Mediterranean countries and eastern Europe. This bushy

Gypsophila paniculata

flower was first cultivated in Great Britain in 1759. It is now probably the most popular filler for bouquets, and in small quantities can be used very successfully to lighten arrangements.

Use in combination with large-headed flowers such as Scabious and Matthiola.

Season: All year round. Peak period April – September.

Available in: White, sometimes pink. Sometimes it can also be found dyed in other colors.

Lasting time: 7 – 14 days.

Flowers: Loose panicles of many tiny, star-like flowers. Choose when most of the flowers on the stem are open.

Stems: Very thin, delicate, branched stems of 12 – 30" (30 – 76 cm).

Special notes: Very suitable for air-drying. Gypsophila is one of the most commonly available of the ready-dried flowers to be found at florists.

Gypsophila is sensitive to ethylene gas and should be kept away from mature fruit and vegetables, dying flowers, and excess heat.

HELENIUM
SNEEZEWEED

H. autumnale; and hybrids.

A popular, summer-garden flower, Helenium is native to the USA and cultivated in Europe (predominantly in Germany and Holland).

Season: July – October.

Available in: Reddish-brown, yellow; with a dark central disc.

Lasting time: 8 – 10 days.

Flowers: These daisy-like flowers have prominent central discs and irregular petals, which tend to splay backwards towards the stem. Approximately 2" (5 cm) across, they form at the end of each branch off a single stem. Choose when most of the flowers on a stem are open.

Stems: Branched, single stems of 12 – 24" (30 – 60 cm).

Helenium autumnale

HELIANTHUS
SUNFLOWER

H. annuus hybrids, *H. decapetalus, H. multiflorus, H. laetiflorus.*

Helianthus comes from the Greek *helios* meaning "sun," and *anthos* meaning "flower." This beautiful, bold flower was cultivated by the North American Indians and is still grown for its seeds and the oil they produce. The perennial *H. multiflorus* "Loddon Gold" has long-lasting double flowers, and the semi-double "Soleil d'Or" is also very popular. The most frequently cultivated, single-flowered cultivar is "Monarch." Combining sunflowers with other brightly-colored, bold flowers – such as orange lilies and red Gerberas – can create a striking focal point, especially in a largely white or monochrome room.

Helianthus annuus

Season: July – October.
Available in: Typically yellow with a brown or maroon center.
Lasting time: 6 – 10 days.
Flowers: Singly borne, long-petalled, daisy-like flowers – some of which can be as much as 10" (25 cm) in diameter. Some semi-double and double forms exist.
Stems: 20 – 40" (50 – 101 cm).
Special notes: Helianthus are suitable for drying, although some petals may drop off.

HELICHRYSUM
EVERLASTING FLOWER, STRAW FLOWER

H. bracteatum.

Originating from Australia, these flowers are widely cultivated across Europe. Their petals have a crisp, papery texture even before they are dried. Their name originates from the Greek *helix,* "spiral" and *khrusos,* "gold."

Season: July – October.
Available in: Most colors, except blue. Often the color on the reverse side of the petal is a different shade.

Helichrysum bracteatum

Lasting time: 10 – 20 days.
Flowers: Showy and daisy-like, these are small and double-flowered, with papery petals.
Stems: 12 – 20" (30 – 50 cm).
Special notes: Helichrysum is one of the most commonly available of the ready-dried flowers to be found at florists, and can sometimes be found dyed in different colors. It is very suitable for drying and thence much used in winter flower arrangements.

Heliconia psittacorum

HELICONIA
LOBSTER CLAW, PARROT FLOWER, FIREBIRD, WILD PLANTAIN

H. andromeda, H. bihai, H. caribaea, H. elongata, H. humilis, H. ivorea, H. magnifica, H. pendula, H. psittacorum, H. rostrata; and many species.

There are many species of Heliconia, and they can be divided into erect and drooping flowers. The erect *H. psittacorum* is the most commonly seen, but *H. magnifica,* for example, has pendent flowers on very tall stems. Related to the banana, they are cultivated in tropical South America and Africa, although there is also some production in temperate countries within hot houses. These are striking flowers and best displayed alone, in a small number, for a bold effect.

Season: Most of the year, but peaking between June and October.
Available in: Red, orange, yellow (*H. psittacorum*). Also pink and lavender.
Lasting time: A long cut life of between 10 and 21 days.
Flowers: Large, bright, waxy bracts hold the flowers inside. Once the flower has been cut, there is no further development of the bracts.
Stems: There is a large range in stem lengths, depending on the species. *H. psittacorum*, for example, are between 12″ and 24″ (30 – 60 cm) tall. In general, however, stem lenghts range from 20 – 60″ (50 – 152 cm).
 The stems are leafless.
Special notes: The stem thicknesses of Heliconia vary, but the strongest, longer-lasting varieties are those with thicker stems.

HELLEBORUS
CHRISTMAS ROSE, LENTEN ROSE, HELLEBORE

H. lividus (*corsicus*), *H. niger*, *H. orientalis*; and hybrids.

Single rows of small petals on leafless stems make Helleborus resemble a tiny wild rose. They are used essentially in Christmas decorations, particularly in Scandinavia. *H. niger* is the Christmas rose, and *H. orientalis* the Lenten rose.

Season: November – January.
Available in: Bright white, maturing to purple (*H. niger*). Green to cream (*H. lividus*). Cream, marked with purple and spotted (*H. orientalis*).
Lasting time: A fairly short life of just 5 – 7 days.
Flowers: Saucer-shaped, single flowers of 1½ – 2″ (4 – 6 cm) across. *H. lividus* types have flowers in clusters. Choose when the petals have opened.
Stems: 8 – 10″ (20 – 25 cm).
Special notes: To prolong cut life, stand flowers in deep, lukewarm water for 6 – 8 hours before arranging.

Helleborus niger

HIPPEASTRUM
AMARYLLIS, BELLADONNA LILY

Hippeastrum hybrids.

Hippeastrum means "horseman star" (from *hippeus*, "knight" and *astron*, "star"), indicating the star-shape of these flowers originally found in southern and central America and the Caribbean. Hippeastrum are often sold as Amaryllis. In fact, Amaryllis is the name given to hybrids of certain Hippeastrum species. The most important varieties are "Red Lion" (red), "Appleblossom" (pink/white) and "Christmas Gift" (white). The true Amaryllis is *Amaryllis belladonna*, but is not common as a cut flower.

Season: Most of the year. Peak period February – March.
Available in: Shades of red, orange, pink, lavender, white, and two-color.
Lasting time: 7 – 14 days.
Flowers: 3 or 4 large, funnel-shaped, outward-facing flowers, approximately 5″ (13 cm) in

White *Freesia*, the short and delicate stems of *Myosotis*, and fragrant branches of *Syringa*, make a sweet-smelling combination for late Spring.

A simple bunch of *Narcissi* is made more individual and special when tied together with strands of garden raffia.

length, are to be found on one stem. These are sometimes striped or frilled. They may be selected when in bud, but only where they show strong color.

Stems: Stout, hollow stems of 12 – 24" (30 – 61 cm). The stem ends tend to splay out when standing in water. This will not affect the life of the flower, but can disturb an arrangement. It can be rectified by wrapping a piece of clear adhesive tape around the end of each stem.

Hippeastrum hybrid

Special notes: The open flowers bruise very easily, and are sensitive to temperatures below 15° C.

A fully mature flower head is very top heavy, but the stem can be made more rigid by inserting a thin stick inside it to give support.

---

have sprung up where he fell, and Apollo named it in memory of his friend. Common as pot plants, these heavily-scented flowers are gaining popularity as cut flowers, especially for late winter and early spring brides.

Season: November – March.
Available in: Violet, blue, crimson, pink, cream, white.
Lasting time: 7 – 14 days.
Flowers: Spikes of tubular flowers, 4 – 6" (10 – 15 cm) long. Depending on the bulb from which they come, flower heads may be heavy and full or tightly packed and graceful. Select when the lower petals are starting to open.
Stems: 8 – 12" (20 – 30 cm).
Special notes: Keep very cool, and mist regularly for increased longevity.

Hyacinthus orientalis

HYACINTHUS
COMMON HYACINTH, DUTCH HYACINTH

H. orientalis hybrids.

Hyachinthus is the Latin translation from the Greek *Huakinthos*, the name of the young man in Greek mythology who was loved by Apollo, but who was fatally struck at a discus-throwing event. A flower was supposed to

---

HYDRANGEA
COMMON HYDRANGEA, FRENCH HORTENSIA

H. macrophylla, H. paniculata.

Hydrangea is very common as a pot plant, and is growing in popularity as a cut flower. Hydrangea originated in Japan and has been cultivated in Europe since 1788, where it remains a favorite garden shrub. It is

Hydrangea species

suitable for adapting to any type of arranging style, but can look particularly effective if the flower heads are cut short and several are placed together in a bowl. For something similar, a combination in a bowl with rose heads, in a matching color, is also effective.

Season: March – September.
Available in: White, pink, blue.
Lasting time: 5 – 10 days.
Flowers: Available in a large range of sizes, star-shaped flowers are borne in wide, terminal flower heads. *H. macrophylla* has a more rounded cluster than the more pyramidal-shaped *H. paniculata*. Choose when the florets are opening.
Stems: 16 – 20″ (40 – 50 cm).
Special notes: Suitable for drying.

HYPERICUM
ST JOHN'S WORT

H. elatum.

The ornamental quality of this shrub is produced by the reddish-brown berries which follow the small, yellow flowers. Hypericum is mainly cultivated in Holland where it is a popular filler for bouquets and arrangements.

Season: September – November.
Available in: Shades of yellow flowers, followed by yellow and reddish-brown berries.
Lasting time: 10 – 12 days. The life of the flowers is only about 5 days.
Flowers: Cup-shaped, often opening out flat and having a central boss of golden stamens. Each flower is approximately 1″ (2.5 cm) wide, appearing at the ends of the many short branchlets.
Stems: Branching, 20 – 24″ (50 – 60 cm).
Special notes: The red and yellow berries make attractive branches for offsetting flowers, or as part of a foliage arrangement.

Hypericum elatum

IRIS
IRIS

I. germanica, I. sibirica, I reticulata, I. x *hollandica* hybrids.

In Greek mythology Iris is the messenger of the gods, and the word itself means "rainbow." These bulbs are largely cultivated in the UK, Holland, and the Channel Islands. Dutch

Iris species

Clear blue *Muscari*, with delicate yellow *Primula*, create a pretty spring posy – held together with bunches of leaves and surrounded by a protective lace collar.

bulbous Iris are the most commonly found, but there are also dwarf varieties (*I. reticulata*) and different categorizations based on variations in shape. Iris are distinctive and dignified flowers, suited to massed traditional designs; as a focal flower in a stark contemporary arrangement; or best of all, perhaps, displayed alone. Some have a noticeable scent, while other varieties have none.

Season: Limited availability all year. The peak period, however, is between March and May.
Available in: Shades of blue and purple with yellow stripes, white with yellow stripes, and yellow with white stripes.
Lasting time: 4 – 8 days.
Flowers: Sword-shaped and usually carried in a fan-like arrangement, the grouping of the two sets of petals creates the characteristic flower shape. The average size of each flower is about 4" (10 cm). The flowers will continue to open in water, but select when there is color already showing, especially during the winter months. Check that closed flowers do not appear dry at their tips, for these will not open.
Stems: 16 – 24" (40 – 60 cm). Tiny *I. reticulata* is on 4 – 8" (10 – 20 cm) stems. Remove any white section of the stem before arranging.
Special notes: Iris are sensitive to ethylene gas and should be kept away from mature fruit and vegetables, dying flowers, and excess heat.

A cool atmosphere will help to prolong vase life, and warmth will encourage buds to open. If they do not open readily, remove the bracts around the flowers.

Ixia species

(cream). Ixia are also commonly kept as pot plants.

Season: April – July.
Available in: White, cream, pink, red, purple, orange.
Lasting time: 7 – 10 days.
Flowers: Ornamental, star-shaped flowers of about 1" (2.5 cm) in diameter, with petals surrounding a dark center. Always choose flowers where all the buds show color.
Stems: Thin. 14 – 18" (35 – 45 cm).
Special notes: Ixia are sensitive to ethylene gas and should be kept away from mature fruit and vegetables, dying flowers, and excess heat.

IXIA
AFRICAN CORN LILY, FLAME OF THE FOREST

I. coccinea, I. javaanica, I macrothyrsa; and hybrids.

Indigenous to South Africa, Ixia belong to the *Iridaceae* family, which includes Iris and Gladioli. Commonly-cultivated varieties include "Titia" (deep pink) and "Hogarth"

KNIPHOFIA
RED-HOT POKER, TORCH LILY, POKER PLANT

K. uvaria hybrids.

Kniphofia is another lily which originates from southern and eastern Africa, but is now widely-cultivated outdoors in Europe. "Royal Standard" is one of the most popular varieties and is sulphur-yellow and red in color. The thicker-stemmed, large-flowered varieties make excellent, bold cut flowers, while the smaller-flowered varieties are useful in traditional arrangements. Cut the length off the stem for smaller designs.

Season: May – October.
Available in: Yellow, orange, red, two-color.
Lasting time: 7 – 10 days.
Flowers: Each smooth, erect flower stem terminates in a poker-like spike of closely-set, tubular flowers with open ends pointing downwards. Cut individual dead flowers from the stem using scissors. Select when the lower florets are opening, for the flowers will continue to open in water.
Stems: Sturdy, slightly curved stems of 12 – 30" (30 – 76 cm).
Special notes: Buy Kniphofia when the lower flowers of the torch are open or about to open.

Kniphofia uvaria

LATHYRUS
SWEET PEA, EVERLASTING PEA

L. odoratus hybrids.

Lathyrus odoratus

Odoratus is Latin for "well scented," and sweet pea have been prized by gardeners for their delicious fragrance for centuries. The older varieties have the best scent; modern varieties are fragrant, but less so. Originating from Italy and Sicily, these flowers are commercially cultivated both outdoors and in greenhouses. They look best arranged alone in a bunch or as an adjunct to a focal flower in a larger design.

Season: April – August.
Available in: Numerous colors, including red, orange, cream, white, and shades of pink and blue.
Lasting time: 6 –10 days.
Flowers: Soft-textured, with butterfly-shaped petals and a very delicate frilled, or sometimes fluted, appearance. An average of 4 or 5, 1"- (2.5 cm-) wide flowers are to be found, well

The easiest of springtime arrangements – single-headed "daffodil" *Narcissi* always look superb displayed together in a good-sized bunch.

An alternative way of displaying *Lavatera* – usually shown in tall, arching branches – is as a small posy of flowers with stems cut short to give a greater intensity of color.

spaced, on each stem. Choose when the lower flower is open and the buds show good color.

Stems: Slender. 10 – 20″ (25 – 50 cm).

Special notes: Keep cool for maximum longevity.

Lathyrus is sensitive to ethylene gas and should be kept away from mature fruit and vegetables, dying flowers, and excess heat.

LAVANDULA
LAVENDER

L. angustifolia, L. dentata, L. x intermedia, L. spica, L. stoechas.

Although the individual flowers are very small, this flower is popular because it is a familiar garden flower with a distinct perfume. *L. intermedia* is an important source of oil for perfume. *L. angustifolia* is the most popular lavender, but *L. dentata* (French lavender), with finely cut leaves, and *L. stoechas* (Spanish lavender), with large flowers, are also good for arrangements.

Season: June – September.

Available in: Gray-blue, and occasionally in white and pink.

Lasting time: 8 – 10 day

Flowers: Borne in slender spikes, up to 2½″ (6 cm) long. Choose when the flowers on the spike are open.

Stems: Leafless stems of between 16″ and 20″ (40 – 50 cm) in length.

Special notes: Very suitable for drying, since Lavandula keeps its color well. Stems should be hung, tied in bunches, in a cool, airy place to dry before the blooms are fully open. Because it retains its scent so well after drying, lavender is frequently used in sachets and pot-pourri. Lavender is one of the most commonly available of the ready-dried flowers to be found at florists.

Lavandula species

LAVATERA
MALLOW

L. trimestris hybrids.

Resembling the wild flowers of the same name, and to which they are related, Lavatera have become a popular summer flower, and unlike many cultivated flowers they have retained a lot of fleshy, lush leaves. They lend themselves well to large arrangements and simple, massed grouping.

Season: June – September.

Available in: Pink, white.

Lasting time: 6 – 8 days.

Flowers: Large, single, trumpet-shaped flowers, 3 – 4″ (7 – 10 cm) wide.

Choose Lavatera where the flowers have started to open.

Stems: 15 – 24″ (38 – 61 cm).

Special notes: The buds of Lavatera continue to develop even after the stems have been cut, and will open in water.

Lavatera trimestris

LEUCADENDRON
SILVER TREE, SAFARI SUNSET, FLAME TIP

Leucadendron species

L. argenteum, L. coniferum, L. discolor, L. eucalyptifolium, L. linifolium, L. salignum.

A South African shrub from the Protea family, now grown in Hawaii, California, and Australia. *L. argenteum* (Silver Tree) has pale, silvery-green leaves and bracts. *L. salignum* varieties have red bracts, while others, such as *L. discolor* and *L. platyspermum*, are pink or yellow. Female branches often have round cones, of various sizes, that will last many weeks.

Season: All year round, but availability is limited in summer.
Available in: Pink, red, orange.
Lasting time: 14 – 28 days.
Flowers: The terminal leaves, virtually concealing the flower, are actually a colorful bract. The male flower is small, while the female is formed as a cone.
Stems: Stem length varies considerably with the varieties, and ranges from 20 – 32" (50 – 81 cm).
Special notes: Suitable for drying.

LEUCOSPERMUM
NODDING PINCUSHION, SUNBURST PROTEA, PINCUSHION PROTEA

L. catherinae, L. conocarpodendron, L. cordifolium, L. cuneiforme, L. erubescens, L. lineare, L. pattersonni, L. reflexum, L. truncatum; and cultivars.

Another South African shrub of the Protea family, which is now grown in Australia and Israel. Leucospermum can develop a slight, honey-like scent in the sunshine. The long, arched stigma provides the decorative quality of these exotic flowers. *L. catherinae* are also known as Pinwheels.

Leucospermum species

Season: All year round. Limited availability in summer.
Available in: Orange, red, pink, yellow. Sometimes they are tinted to enhance the tones.
Lasting time: Approximately 14 days.
Flowers: The size of the flower head ranges from 2 – 5" (5 – 13 cm), with styles forming a dome. Flowers are formed singly at the end of each stem. Be sure to select where the flowers have a bushy, spiny look.
Stems: Woody stems of 16 – 24" (40 – 60 cm).
Special notes: These are fairly delicate flowers and need careful handling.

Liatris spicata

LIATRIS
GAY FEATHER, BUTTON SNAKEROOT, KANSAS FEATHER, KANSAS GODFATHER, BLAZING STAR

L. pycnostachya, L. spicata; and hybrids.

Spicata means "spike-shaped," and accurately describes the densely-covered tubular spires. Liatris originates from the eastern part of the USA and has been cultivated in Europe since the eighteenth century.

Season: All year round.
Available in: Mauve, pink, cream-white.
Lasting time: 10 – 14 days.
Flowers: These are feathery and thistle-like, but densely-borne on wand-like spikes. Choose stems where the first top florets are open. Select spikes with at least 2" (5 cm) of flowers open. It is unlikely that all the flowers on the spike will open.
Stems: Upright, leafless stems of 24 – 32" (60 – 80 cm). "Kobold" is a dwarf variety with 15 – 18" (38 – 46 cm) stems.
Special notes: Liatris flowers mature from the top downwards, which is very uncommon.

Suitable for drying.

LILIUM
LILY

L. auratum, *L. candidum*, *L. longiflorum*, Mid-century (Asian hybrids), Oriental hybrids, *L. speciosum*.

Elegant and sophisticated, lilies are one of the most popular contemporary flowers, and commercial growers are developing new varieties every year. Their popularity can be attributed to their longevity, and to their sometimes opulent perfume.

Lilies are often sold by the single stem. Choose when several flowers are open and other buds are ripe and showing good color. Flowers that are discolored or transparent are well past their best.

To increase longevity, lower blooms and wilted leaves should be carefully removed, encouraging the upper buds to open. Sometimes the petals may need careful teasing out.

Remove the white section of the stem, which is not good at taking up water. Flower food in very small quantities is useful, but it can discolor leaves if used in larger amounts.

Lilies should always be handled very carefully, as they bruise and discolor extremely easily.

Because the pollen can stain clothing, soft furnishings, and the petals of the flower itself, you may prefer to remove the prominent stamens by snipping them out.

The orange Tiger Lily (*L. tigrinum*) is similar in shape to *L. speciosum*, only smaller.

MADONNA LILIES

L. candidum.

Native to the eastern Mediterranean, this is one of the most beautiful and best-loved of lilies. It is very fragrant.

Season: All year round, but peak period June – July.
Available in: White with yellow anthers.
Lasting time: 10 – 14 days.
Flowers: Trumpet shaped, 3 – 3½" (8 – 9 cm) long.
Stems: Up to 60" (150 cm).

Lilium candidum

EASTER LILIES, BERMUDA LILIES

L. longiflorum.

Longiflorum literally means "long flowered." These are striking flowers and look stunning displayed alone, or as the focal point of an arrangement. They are ideal for tall, floor-

Lilium longiflorum

Astrantia, Alchemilla mollis and *Lonicera* showing natural beauty in a casual window sill arrangement catching the early morning light.

standing arrangements, and are often used to decorate churches at Easter time. They have a distinctive, sweet fragrance. A member of the *L. auratum* family, the largest of all the lilies, they have white, hanging flowers with orange or yellow stripes and flecks.

Season: All year round, but especially in late spring and early summer.
Available in: Pure white, with bright yellow pollen.
Lasting time: 8 – 14 days.
Flowers: The long, trumpet-shaped flowers grow sideways from the stalk, with between 1 and 6 flowers per stem, each 5 – 7" (12 – 18 cm) in length.
Stems: Thick, strong stems up to 60" (150 cm).

MID-CENTURY LILIES, ASIAN HYBRIDS

Mid-century hybrids originate from crossing hybrids of *L. hollandium* and *L. tigrinum.* They are seldom fragrant. These are typically sold by the stem. "Enchantment," in orange, and "Conneticut King," in yellow, are especially popular varieties.

Season: All year round.
Available in: Many color varieties, ranging from lemon-yellow through shades of orange, to crimson and red, speckled with maroon or brown; and white.
Lasting time: 10 – 14 days.
Flowers: These are borne singly or in umbels of up to 12 upright flowers. Each cup-shaped flower head may be 4 – 5" (10 – 13 cm) wide. They are mainly upright, but can be pendent, and have recurved petal tips.
Stems: Strong, erect stems up to 40" (100 cm).
Special notes: Asian hybrids are the most cultivated lily, and are considerably cheaper than the Oriental hybrid lilies.

Unlike other lilies, Asian hybrids are sensitive to ethylene gas and should be kept away from mature fruit and vegetables, dying flowers, and excess heat.

ORIENTAL HYBRID LILIES, TRUMPET LILIES

An ever-expanding group of exotic lilies, with pendent, cup-shaped flowers. They originate from crosses with *L. auratum, L. speciosum,* and

Mid-century *Lilium*

Oriental-hybrid *Lilium*

Lilium speciosum

L. rubrum. Typically sold by the stem, the upright, pink variety "Stargazer" is a very popular example.

Season: All year round, with a peak period in September and October.
Available in: Predominantly white or pink flowers, with distinctive stripes or speckling. Popular varieties include "Casablanca" (white), "Stargazer" (striped pink), "Le rêve" (pale pink), and "Furore" (smaller, with white flowers).
Lasting time: 10 – 15 days, with new buds opening throughout this time. The foliage may die slightly earlier than the flowers.
Flowers: Usually pendent, these cup-shaped lilies, with recurved petals, are up to 8" (20 cm) across. There are up to 3 flowers per stem.
Stems: Range from 36 – 48" (90 – 120 cm).
Special notes: It is advisable to remove the anthers from the stamens if the flowers are to be used in bouquets, as the heavy pollen can stain clothes and furnishings.

SPECIOSUM LILIES

L. speciosum.

Speciosum means "showy," and these dramatic lilies are crown-shaped with distinctively-marked, recurved petals and long stamens. The flower heads hang down from individual stems which grow at irregular intervals from the main, curved stalk. The white "Album" and pink "Uchida" are popular.

Season: All year round, with a peak period in the late summer and autumn.
Available in: Shades of pink, and white.
Lasting time: 10 – 15 days.
Flowers: These are bowl-shaped, 3 – 5" (8 – 13 cm) long, with recurved, waxy petals.
Stems: Up to 48" (150 cm).
Special notes: With their rather straggly growing habits, these lilies need special care to avoid stems getting tangled up together. It is advisable to remove the anthers if the flowers are to be used in bouquets.

LIMONIUM
SEA LAVENDER, STATICE

L. ferulaceum, L. incanum, L. latifolium, L perezii, L. sinuatum, L. suworowii, L. tatarica; and many hybrids.

Originating from the Caucasus, Limonium was first cultivated in Britain in 1791. It is a popular filler for bouquets of both fresh and dried flowers. *L. latifolium* is known as Sea lavender, and has small mauve flowers.

Limonium latifolium

Limonium ferulaceum

Limonium sinuatum

Limonium suworowii

Combined with other blue or mauve flowers, for example *Centurea cyanus*, it makes a beautifully soft-colored, understated arrangement. "Karel de Groot" is the most common variety of the *L. ferulaceum* variety of Limonium. It has a pyramidal-shaped branch and is a little taller than other cultivars. *L. suworowii*, known as Russian statice or Rat's tail statice, originates from Turkestan. It is visually very different from the other varieties of the genus, having long spikes that naturally curl over.

German statice (*L. tatarica*) is also indigenous to Turkestan. It has been cultivated in Europe since the nineteenth century (hence its common name) and has now naturalized in the countries surrounding both the Mediterranean and Aegean. *L. sinuatum* is the common statice.

Season: All year round.

Available in: Pale pink, pale mauve. Other colors are available where the Limonium has been dyed.

Lasting time: 10 -16 days.

Flowers: Tiny, individual, funnel-shaped flowers are crowded together on spikes or in panicles.

Stems: 12 – 28" (30 – 70 cm), depending on the variety.

Special notes: If Limonium is kept in a confined and damp or humid space, it can become very smelly.

Once the flowers are open, Limonium is one of the easiest and most successful flowers for drying. For air-drying, tie the stems in bundles and hang upside down.

LUPINUS
LUPINE

L. polyphyllus hybrids.

Originating from California and south-west Canada, lupins were first cultivated in Great Britain in 1826 by George Russell, a Yorkshire gardener, and have since naturalized in many parts of Europe. The name derives from the Latin *lupinus*, meaning "wolfish," from the belief that the plant ravenously exhausted the soil. They are very effective arranged in a vase without accompanying flowers or foliage, but look good in a country-garden arrangement.

Season: May – August.

Available in: Violet-blue, pink, red, yellow, white, and often two-color.

Both *Crocosmia* and *Artemisia* foliage are available from late June until September, and complement each other in this arrangement inspired by the colors of fall.

Lasting time: 5 – 7 days.

Flowers: Pea-shaped flowers are carried densely in slender, spine-like racemes. Choose where most of the flowers on the spike have started to open.

Stems: Thin stems of 24 – 32″ (60 – 80 cm). Lupin stems are hollow. They should be filled with water and, with a finger used to cover the end, stood in the vase to prevent an air-lock forming.

Special notes: Lupins will wilt very quickly if left out of water for any length of time. However, filling the stems with water, as advised above, will help to prolong their life.

Lysimachia clethroides

Lupinus polyphyllus

LYSIMACHIA
LOOSE STRIFE

L. clethroides, L. punctata.

Named after Lysimachus, a Macedonian general under Alexander the Great (360 – 281 BC) and later King of Thrace, who is said to have discovered the genus. This shrubby summer plant is cultivated in Europe, outdoors.

Season: July – September.

Available in: White. *L. punctata* has larger, yellow flowers.

Lasting time: 7 – 9 days.

Flowers: The arching nature of the flower's racemes is a typical feature. Each spike is approximately 3 – 4″ (7 – 10 cm) long, and packed with tiny, star-shaped flowers. Select when the flowers are starting to open.

Stems: 24 – 28″ (60 – 70 cm).

Special notes: Avoid excess heat and placing in direct sunlight, and keep an eye on vase water level.

MAHONIA
OREGON GRAPE, HOLLYGRAPE,
BARBERRY

M. aquifolium, M. japonica.

Originating from North America, and named after the American botanist Bernard Mcmahon

Mahonia aquifolium (flowers)

Mahonia aquifolium (fruits)

(d.1816), Mahonia is a shrub cultivated all over Europe, and used particularly at Christmas, when it bears clusters of blue-black berries. Fragrant flowers appear in spring.

Season: Berries are present all year round, but the flowers only appear between April and May.

Available in: Yellow flowers, blue-black berries.

Lasting time: 14 – 21 days. Flower life only about 7 days.

Flowers: Clusters of bell-shaped or globular flowers, approximately 3 – 5" across, form drooping panicles. Choose where flower buds are showing color.

Stems: 16 – 24" (40 – 60 cm).

Special notes: The leaves, composed of between 5 and 9 holly-like, spiny, glossy leaflets, look wonderful in foliage arrangements, and will last for about a week without water.

MATTHIOLA
STOCK, GILLYFLOWER

M. incana hybrids.

Named after Dr Matthiole (1527 – 1576), who was personal physician to Emperor Maximillian of Austria and wrote several medical and botanical books, Matthiola has been cultivated for centuries, and originates from the Mediterranean countries. Matthiola has a very strong, pungent perfume. The bold form of these flowers makes them suitable for the largest of arrangements, and they can look wonderful in combination with roses in a matching color.

Season: Most of the year. Although greenhousing means that Matthiola can be available all year round, the peak period is between May and September, since this is its natural season.

Available in: White, red, pink, cream, lilac, purple, yellow.

Lasting time: 7 – 10 days

Flowers: 1"- (2.5 cm-) wide flowers are borne

In an arrangement resonant of the past, mix *Paeonia* and *Rosa* – two of the most popular flowers available – for unashamed indulgence in soft textures.

Matthiola incana

in compact 6 – 9″ (15 – 23 cm) spikes. Select when about half the flowers on the spike are open.

Stems: Woody stems, from 12 – 28″ (30 – 70 cm).

Special notes: The stems exude slime which will pollute the vase water, so change water frequently, adding more flower food.

Longevity will be helped if Matthiola are kept cool and foliage below water level is removed. In addition, keep out of direct sunlight, heat, and draughts.

MOLUCCELLA
BELLS OF IRELAND, SHELL FLOWER

M. laevis.

Moluccella used to be eaten as a vegetable, and has been cultivated in Europe since the sixteenth century. The flowers are faintly fragrant with a peppery perfume. Unusual and attractive, Moluccella also looks good dried,

for a winter decoration. The noticeable part of the plant is the papery green cup around each bloom.

Season: All year round. Peak period April – August.

Available in: Green with white flowers.

Lasting time: 8 – 12 days.

Flowers: Tall flower spikes. The tiny flowers are white and insignificant, but the bright green, bell-shaped calyxes give Moluccella its decorative quality.

Stems: 15 – 32″ (38 – 80 cm).

Special notes: Cutting the stems every couple of days often prevents the stem tips from drooping.

Moluccella laevis

MUSCARI
GRAPE HYACINTH

M. armeniacum. M. botryoides, M. comosum.

Originally from the Balkans, Greece, and Asia, this bulb is mainly cultivated in Holland. The name is derived from the word "musk," due to the faint scent these flowers have. Some cultivars have double flowers. *M. comosum* has a fluffy, lavender-colored form called "Plumosum."

Muscari species

Season: December – April.
Available in: Violet-blue, white.
Lasting time: 4 – 8 days.
Flowers: Clusters of tiny, tubular flowers on terminal spikes. Choose when some of the lower florets are just opening.
Stems: Thin, short stems of 4 – 8" (10 – 20 cm).
Special notes: Keep away from excess heat and direct sunlight.
    Suitable for drying.

MYOSOTIS
FORGET-ME-NOT

Myosotis hybrids.

Myosotis comes from the Greek *muosotis,* meaning "mouse ear," and refers to the furriness of the leaves. These flowers originate from Europe and northern Asia and are a popular garden flower. Because of their small size, they have limited use in arrangements, but they are ideal for a small posy or dressing-table arrangement.

Season: April – August.
Available in: Mainly blue, some pink, and some white.
Lasting time: 7 – 10 days.
Flowers: Small and salver-shaped.
Stems: 12 – 16" (30 – 40 cm).
Special notes: Myosotis tend to lose their color as they age.

Myosotis species

NARCISSUS
NARCISSUS, DAFFODIL, JONQUIL

Narcissus hybrids.

Narcissus comes from the Greek *narkissos,* meaning "numbness" – a reference, perhaps, to the narcotic properties attributed to the species. It was the name of the youth transformed by the gods into a flower because of his acute self-obsession. The Romans first cultivated the wild Narcissus, and they have remained an extremely popular flower, from which new varieties appear every year. They are mainly cultivated in areas of Great Britain, the Channel Islands, and Holland. Daffodils, although seasonal, are amongst the top five most cultivated and popular flowers. They

The lilac-pink "Silver Star" *Rosa* is a popular and fragrant variety and is elegantly complemented by the luxuriant grey-green leaves of *Eucalyptus*.

Narcissus hybrid (single-headed, trumpet)

Narcissus hybrid (single-headed)

can look especially good in a clear glass vase and wonderful in a general arrangement of spring flowers. Combine yellow Narcissi with orange Ranunculus for a warm spring combination.

The family of Narcissi can be divided into eight major groups, which are distinguished by their flower shape (see below). To summarize, the simplest way of categorizing these is to notice if the flower head is single- or double-flowered, i.e. has one row of petals surrounding the corona (trumpet) or many; and to distinguish between those with one flower head per stem or several.

Season: October – April, with a peak period between January and March.
Available in: Shades of yellow, white, and two-color with yellow or white petals and orange, apricot, or pink coronas.
Lasting time: They have a relatively short vase life of only about 5 days, but can be bought in green bud, which gives extra days as the flowers mature and open.
Flowers: TRUMPET: Primarily with a single head per stem, these flowers have a corona (trumpet) as long as, or longer than, the petals. Daffodils are examples of Trumpet Narcissi.
LARGE COROLLA: Single flowers on each

stem, which have a corona at least a third the length of the petals.
SHORT COROLLA: Usually single flowers, where the corona is less than one third the length of the petals.
DOUBLE-FLOWERED: Single flowers per stem, where the petal and cup structure is replaced by multiple petals.

Narcissus hybrid (double flowered)

Narcissus hybrid (Polyanthus)

JONQUIL: Sweetly-scented, multiple flower heads per stem, where the corona is short and the petals are often fairly flat, broad, and slightly rounded.

POLYANTHUS: Multi-headed stems with double-type petals.

SPLIT COROLLA: One flower per stem, where the corona is flat and deeply cut.

TAZETTA: Sweetly-fragrant flowers in clusters of 12 or more, with straight-sided coronas.

POET'S NARCISSUS: Small, colored corona with white petals.

Stems: 6 – 20" (15 – 50 cm).

Special notes: Narcissi emit a latex from their stems when cut, which is known as "daffodil slime" and is harmful to other flowers. Generally, therefore, either keep daffodils separate or use the special cut-flower food which makes them safe to mix with other flowers. Alternatively, keep the Narcissi separately in water for 24 hours before combining with other flowers in fresh water. Do not cut anything further from the stem ends at this point.

NERINE
SPIDER LILY, GUERNSEY LILY

N. bowdenii, N. flexuosa, N. sarniensis, N. undulata (N. crispa).

Although nerines were originally just an autumn bulb, modern bulb-freezing techniques now make them available for most of the year. The furled nature of the petals of these graceful flowers well suits their arrangement with the contrasting shape of roses. *N. undulata* is a smaller variety.

Season: Most of the year, but mainly late summer and autumn.

Available in: Shades of pink, from pale to dark, and some a rich red or orange-hued; white.

Lasting time: 12 – 14 days.

Flowers: Elegant clusters of curled flowers form a flower head approximately 5" (13 cm) across. Flowers should be selected when all the buds are well developed and just about to open.

Stems: Bare, straight, leafless stems of approximately 12 – 24" (30 – 61cm).

Special notes: Nerines prefer a cool temperature, but exposure to cold will cause the flower heads to turn slightly blue.

Nerine bowdenii

NIGELLA
LOVE-IN-THE-MIST, DEVIL-IN-THE-BUSH

N. damascena.

The feathery foliage and striking seed pod make these noticeably individual flowers. Nigella is the diminutive of the Latin *niger*, meaning "black," and refers to the tiny black seeds of the spherical seed heads which are frequently used in dried-flower arrangements and bouquets. The delicate fern-like foliage has the effect of lightening an arrangement.

Season: June – August/September.

Available in: Pale blue; occasionally white, pink, mauve.

Nigella damascena

Lasting time: 7 – 10 days.
Flowers: Single, saucer-shaped, papery flowers, with a striking, egg-shaped seed pod. The single flowers average about 1" (2.5 cm) across.
Stems: Thin, erect stems of 16 – 20" (41 – 50 cm).
Special notes: Nigella seed pods are amongst the most commonly available of the ready-dried flowers to be found at florists.

ONCIDIUM
GOLDEN SHOWER ORCHID

O. pulchellum, O. sphacelatum, O. splendidum, O. varicosum; and hybrids.

The common name refers to the frequently-cultivated variety, although there are many other varieties in the Oncidium genus which originates from South America. The most commonly available types are varieties such as "Golden Shower" and "Goldiana."

Season: All year round.
Available in: Predominantly yellow with brown markings. However, the miniature hybrids come in a wide range of colors.
Lasting time: 10 – 14 days.
Flowers: The average size of each flower is 1 – 2" (2.5 – 5 cm). Miniature hybrids have tiny flowers just ½ – 1" (1 – 2.5 cm) across. Numerous flowers appear along the stem.
Stems: Full-size Oncidium are on approximately 24 – 36" (60 – 91 cm) stems, but miniature hybrids are on just 3 – 15" (7 – 38 cm) stems. The large number of flowers on the wiry, thin stems causes them to arch with the weight.
Special notes: Oncidium are sensitive to ethylene gas and should be kept away from maturing fruit and vegetables, dying flowers, and excess heat.

Like all orchids, Oncidium appreciate being sprayed to maintain moisture levels, and should be kept away from heat and draughts.

Oncidium species

Single-colored *Gerbera* make a striking contrast in a collection of deep blue bottles, and will last longer if kept cool and out of direct sunlight.

ORNITHOGALUM
STAR OF BETHLEHEM

O. arabicum.

Ornithogalum arabicum

The name Ornithogalum means "bird's milk," and was an expression used by the ancient Greeks to describe something amazing. *O. arabicum* has distinctive black ovaries which differentiate it from *O. thrysoides.*

Season: All year round, with a peak period between July and October.
Available in: White, with a black ovary.
Lasting time: 14 – 21 days.
Flowers: The flower head of *O. arabicum* is made up of between 8 and 12 star-shaped florets of 1" (2.5 cm), or more, across. Choose where the lower florets are beginning to open and the majority are showing color.
Stems: Stout, leafless stems of 16 – 36" (40 – 91 cm).
Special notes: Suitable for drying.

CHINCHERINCHEE, WIND LILY

O. thrysoides; and hybrids.

Originating from South Africa, this species is widely cultivated in Holland and the Channel Islands. These flowers have a more spherical shape than *O. arabicum* and will curve towards the light. Stems will keep straight if light is directly above them.

Season: All year round. Peak period July – October.
Available in: White, cream, yellow.
Lasting time: 14 – 21 days.
Flowers: Buds will open over a period of days, but pinching off the top bud will promote the opening of the others.
Stems: Erect stems of 12 – 24" (30 – 60 cm) in height. Avoid buying if the stems are turning yellow, as it may indicate that the flowers will fail to open.
Special notes: They are suitable for drying, and this is when they are often dyed pale blue or pink.

These flowers last longest when kept cool. They are sensitive to ethylene gas and should be kept away from mature fruit and vegetables, dying flowers, and excess heat.

Although erect initially, stems will lean toward light, so they should be turned regularly or placed where the light source is directly above them.

Ornithogalum thrysoides

PAEONIA
PEONY

P. lactiflora, P. suffruticosa and *P. lutea* hybrids.

Originating from Siberia and Mongolia, these sensational flowers have been cultivated in Europe since the beginning of the nineteenth century, where they are prized by gardeners and commercial growers alike. "Sarah Bernhardt" is the popular pink variety, and the white "Duchesse de Nemours" is very fragrant. The soft and silky quality of the petals should be taken into account when choosing flowers to accompany Peonies. *P. suffruticosa* and *P. lutea* hybrids are the tree peonies, which are silky petalled, but do not transport as well as the more commonly available *P. lactiflora*.

Season: June – July.
Available in: Pink, white, lavender.
Lasting time: 5 – 12 days. For the longest vase life, choose peonies where the buds are showing good color but have not yet opened.
Flowers: These showy flowers are rounded to bowl-shaped, and open out almost flat when fully mature. They are available in single, anemone-flowered, and double forms, and each stem carries one flower head. Flowers are

Paeonia lactiflora

from 3 – 5" (8 – 13 cm) across, depending on the variety.
Stems: 16 – 24" (40 – 60 cm).
Special notes: Suitable for drying.

PAPAVER
POPPY, ORIENTAL POPPY, ICELAND POPPY, HEN AND CHICKENS

P. nudicaule, P. orientale, P.somniferum; and hybrids.

Poppies grow all over Europe and eastern Asia, and they have been cultivated since 1730. Most are now grown on the French and Italian Riviera. One of the most popular varieties is "San Remo". The petals themselves have the texture of tissue paper and look delicate but wonderfully bright. These flowers are ideal for loose, open designs. *P. nudicaule* is the Iceland poppy, and *P. somniferum* is known as Hen and Chickens. The field poppy is *P. rhoeas*.

Also used as a cut flower is the California poppy (*Eschscholzia californica*), most commonly to be found in bright orange-yellow, between June and October.

Season: March – August.
Available in: Yellow, cream, orange, pale salmon, white, red.
Lasting time: 5 – 8 days.
Flowers: Cup-shaped blooms are made up of four overlapping petals which taper towards the base. These can eventually open up almost flat, to about 2½" (6 cm) across. Select those with buds just starting to open or, in the case of double types, those recently opened.
Stems: Slender, leafless, long, wiry stems of 16 – 24" (40 – 60 cm). Be sure the stems are in good condition on purchase.
Special notes: *P. somniferum* (Hen and Chickens) provides the dried seed heads which are available all the year round. This is one of the more common flowers to be found on sale at those florists selling dried flowers.

Dipping stem ends in boiling water for 5 seconds will prevent the loss of latex from the stem and early wilting of the flowers.

Papaver orientale

The exotic beauty of a single spray of *Cymbidium* orchid, with a couple of tiny *Anthurium* leaves, is fully appreciated in a narrow bud vase.

Flowers: Just one or two 1 – 2" (2.5 – 5 cm) flowers are to be found on each stem. They are delicately and exotically marked with stripes and spots. Choose when the flowers are open.

Stems: 8 – 10" (20 – 25 cm).

Special notes: They are sensitive to ethylene gas and should be kept away from mature fruit and vegetables, dying flowers, and excess heat.

The upper part of the stem has hairs which should be kept clear of the vase water since, like foliage, they will tend to make the vase water slimy.

Mist regularly with water to maintain humidity.

Paphiopedilum species

PAPHIOPEDILUM
SLIPPER ORCHID, LADY'S SLIPPER ORCHID, CYPRIPEDIUM

P. bellatulum, P. callosum. P. ciliolare. P. fairieanum; and hybrids.

A family of more than 20,000 different varieties, which are bred and grown in both Europe and the USA. Their ancestors can be traced back to Asia, and the first hybrid was cultivated in the UK in 1869. The extended lip of the flower resembles a slipper, hence its common name. The hybrids available are bred for shape and strong colors. These are particularly expensive flowers.

Season: Limited availability all year round, but particularly to be found September – January.

Available in: White, pink, dark red, white, yellow.

Lasting time: 28 – 35 days.

PHALAENOPSIS
MOTH ORCHID, AMABILIS

P. amabilis, P. amboinensis, P. lueddemanniana; and hybrids.

Phalaenopsis means "resembling a moth," hence its common name. One of its ancestors comes from Java, where the leaves are eaten as

Phalaenopsis species

a vegetable. Nowadays, these orchids are a very popular flower for corsages and are available in sprays of up to 15 flowers or as single flowers. The modern hybrids are developed from numerous different species and genera.

Season: All year round.
Available in: Most commonly white, but also yellow, violet, pink.
Lasting time: 7 – 14 days.
Flowers: The flowers are composed of waxy sepals and flat petals. There can be up to 15 flowers carried on each stem, each up to 4" (10 cm) across.
Stems: Thin, branched, arching stems from 16 – 34" (40 – 86 cm).
Special notes: As with all orchids, Phalaenopsis need a cool atmosphere and frequent misting to ensure longevity. They are sensitive to ethylene gas and should be kept away from mature fruit and vegetables, dying flowers, and excess heat.

Handle carefully as Phalaenopsis bruise easily.

PHLOX
SUMMER PHLOX

Phlox hybrids (of *P. arendsii, P. maculata, P. paniculata*).

Via the Latin, from the Greek, Phlox means "plant of glowing color," literally "flame." *P. maculata* and *P. paniculata* hybrids are cultivated in Europe and the USA, and frequently - grown varieties include "Bright Eyes" (pink with darker center), "Rembrandt" (white) and "Alpha" (deep pink). Phlox has a sweet scent which attracts insects. They are ideal for opulent arrangements of mixed summer flowers.
Season: May – October.
Available in: White, pink, pale violet, purple.
Lasting time: 5 – 10 days.
Flowers: Bright clusters of freely-borne, salver-shaped flowers. *P. maculata* has fine, tapering flower spikes, while *P. paniculata* has a domed head with multiple flowers on one

Phlox paniculata

A simple, oblong, glass vase and an uncluttered arrangement bring out the elegance of white *Gladiolus*.

Two stems of *longiflorum Lilium*, with *Anthurium* leaves, make a scented, contemporary arrangement when placed in a simple hand-blown glass vase.

stem. Choose where most of the flowers have opened.

Stems: 15 – 24" (38 – 61 cm).

Special notes: These are very thirsty flowers, so vase water levels should be watched.

Removing some foliage will also help to extend vase life.

Phlox paniculata

Physalis alkekengi

Stems: 20 – 24" (50 – 60 cm).

Special notes: These are very suitable for drying and will last this way for up to two years. Indeed, Physalis is more popular dried than fresh.

PHYSALIS
CHINESE LANTERN, CAPE GOOSEBERRY, BLADDER CHERRY, WINTER CHERRY

P. alkekengi (var. *frachetii*).

Originating from Japan, Physalis means "water blister," and refers to the swollen orange calyxes which it bears.

Season: September – October.

Available in: Orange.

Lasting time: 6 – 10 days.

Flowers: Deep-orange berries encircled by swollen, orange, lantern-shaped calyxes of 2 – 2½" (5 – 6 cm) in diameter.

PHYSOSTEGIA
OBEDIENT PLANT, FALSE DRAGONHEAD

P. virginiana.

Originating from the eastern USA, these fairly fussy flowers can benefit from being displayed alongside plain green foliage.

Season: June – September.

Available in: White, pink, mauve. Sometimes these flowers are dyed and can be found in yellow, green, red, or blue.

Lasting time: 7 – 12 days.

Flowers: The snapdragon-like flowers are closely set to form a spike. Flowers open from the bottom upwards.

Stems: Upright stems of 12 – 24" (30 – 60 cm).

Special notes: If bent slightly, these flowers will remain in an altered position.

Physostegia virginiana

POLIANTHES
TUBEROSE

P. tuberosa.

Tuberose probably originates from Mexico, but it has been cultivated in southern France for centuries for the perfume industry. It has a very heavy, sweet fragrance. Combine, perhaps, with pale lilac and white Amaryllis (Hippeastrum).

Season: Mainly June – September.
Available in: Creamy-white (the buds have a natural-pink exterior tint).
Lasting time: 7 – 14 days.
Flowers: Approximately 1″ (2.5 cm) long, the flowers are borne in thick, erect spikes. The petals grow from a funnel-shaped tube.

Flowers are available in single and double forms. Select when the first flowers are starting to open and the rest are showing color.
Stems: 24 – 32″ (60 – 80 cm).
Special notes: A cool atmosphere will affect the intensity of the fragrance.

Tuberose will bend towards the light, but top buds can be pinched out to avoid this.

Polianthes tuberosa

PROTEA
KING PROTEA, GIANT HONEY POT, SUGAR BUSH, PINK MINK, GIANT WOOLLY BEARD

P. compacta, P. cynaroides, P. grandiceps, P. nerifolia, P. magnifica, P. repens; and some hybrids.

The name Protea comes from the mythic Greek sea god, Proteus, who herded seals for Poseidon and could assume various shapes

Tulipa will naturally curve toward light and look beautiful when unadulterated and left to bend. The shape of parrot *Tulipa* creates extra interest.

Broken-off heads of *Chrysanthemum*, purple *Limonium*, *Alstroemeria* and *Hydrangea* are clustered together in a shallow bowl, filled with well-soaked moss.

Protea nerifolia

at will. The use of his name refers to the many forms of this plant. There are cone, cup, and bowl shapes, with both silky and sticky "beards" inside the bracts.

P. cynaroides is known as "King Protea," and is large, pink, and bowl shaped. *P. magnifica* is "Queen Protea," and is similar, but smaller, and also to be found in white. *P. repens* is known as "sugar bush" or "honey pot," and has a red or white, sticky, cone-shaped flower head up to 6" (15 cm) long. *P. nerifolia*, or "pink mink," is also cone shaped, but slightly smaller than *P. repens*.

Protea are grown in Australia, Hawaii, and California.

Season: All year round. Peak period, September – May.

Available in: Pink, red, white, lavender,

orange; yellow-colored bracts surround the flower.

Lasting time: 14 – 21 days.

Flowers: The flower is surrounded by colorful bracts which slowly open up to give a flower head as much as 10" (25 cm) across, in the case of King Protea. Select while the bracts are still surrounding the flower.

Stems: Woody. 8 – 16" (20 – 40 cm).

Special notes: Before placing in water, remove at least 1" (2.5 cm) from the stem and re-cut every few days, using secateurs. This will prolong vase life.

Leaves will often blacken and consequently Protea may be sold with them already removed.

Suitable for drying.

PRUNUS
FLOWERING CHERRY, FLOWERING ALMOND, FLOWERING PEACH, ORNAMENTAL PLUMS

P. glandulosa, P. triloba, P. persica.

Prunus is the Latin for "plum tree." There are various varieties of blossom appearing on leafless branches, including *P. glandulosa*

Prunus persica

Prunus dulcis

(white almond), *P. triloba* (pink almond), *P. persica* (pink or white peach). These are all the most superb spring blossoms and look good in generous quantities in large arrangements.

Larger branches of locally-grown blossom are available at most flower markets in early spring.

Season: December – April.
Available in: White, pink.
Lasting time: 8 – 14 days.
Flowers: Delicate, cup- or bowl-shaped flowers of five, usually rounded, petals, which often open out flat to between 1" and 2" (2.5 – 5 cm) across. Choose when the flowers are still in bud. Use of flower food in the water will encourage opening.
Stems: Woody. 24 – 39" (60 – 100 cm).
Special notes: Stem ends will benefit from re-cutting. Use secateurs.

RANUNCULUS
PERSIAN RANUNCULUS, FRENCH
BUTTERCUP, TURBAN BUTTERCUP

R. asiaticus.

The genus name is a derivative of the Latin *rana*, meaning "frog," and refers to the swampy places where these flowers are found in the wild. There are four main types: French, Peony-flowered, Persian, and Turban. They all look good in small arrangements. A combination of Ranunculus with tulips in a matching color, perhaps with a foliage such as maidenhair fern, can look beautifully soft.

Season: January – May. Limited availability the rest of the year. (Spring is the main season,

Ranunculus asiaticus

Dianthus caryophyllus in deep reds, mauves and cerise, contrast with spiky flowers of bright pink *Nerines* to bring a modern slant to the much displayed carnation.

but growers force the plants for cut flowers at other times of year too.)

Available in: White, yellow, orange, pink, red.

Lasting time: 5 – 10 days.

Flowers: Bowl-shaped, they often open out almost flat when mature. Modern hybrids have 3" (8 cm), fully double flowers, but varieties can vary in size from between 1" and 4" (2.5 – 10 cm) in diameter. Choose as the flowers are just starting to open out.

Stems: Fine, slender, hollow stems from 10 – 20" (25 – 50 cm) in length.

Special notes: Suitable for drying.

ROSA
ROSE

Rosa hybrids.

Roses are amongst the top five most cultivated and most popular flowers available. *R. chinensis*, known as the Bengal rose, is one of the most important ancestors of today's hybrids and was introduced to Europe from Bengal in 1768. Crossing this rose with *R. gallica*, a native to central Europe, created the Bourbon hybrids. Many other roses have been used to create the thousands of roses being produced by commercial growers and the new varieties which are introduced each year. Indeed, there is such a large range that they are useful in any arrangement. It should be noted, however, that climbing hybrid teas, *floribunda* and *grandiflora* roses, are typically garden roses and less likely to be found in the cut-flower markets.

Scent in commercial cut roses is not common, but there are a few with a very pronounced fragrance, such as "Jacaranda", "Sterling Silver", and "Osiana."

The term "Sweetheart roses" is sometimes used to refer to medium-flowered roses and sometimes to mini roses, so it is safest to describe the size when seeking to buy.

Season: All year round.

Available in: An enormous range of colors,

Rosa hybrid (small flowered)

Rosa hybrid (medium flowered)

Rosa hybrid (large flowered)

virtually everything except blue.

Lasting time: 8 – 18 days.

Flowers: Most of the roses at florists are hybrid tea roses, grown for perfect form and slowly-opening buds, with the longer-stemmed varieties the most valued. For ease of identification, commercially-grown roses can be divided into four main groups:

LARGE-FLOWERED ROSES. These are from 4 – 6" (10 – 15 cm) across, when open, and have a stem length of 14 – 36" (35 – 91 cm). Popular varieties include "Sonia" (deep pink), "Jacaranda" (lilac pink and scented), "Tineke" (white), "Veronica" (pink), "Baccara" (red), "Madame Delbard" (deep red and scented).

MEDIUM-FLOWERED ROSES. The flower head is between 3" and 4" (8 – 10 cm), and the cut-stem length, 10 – 24" (25 – 61 cm). Popular varieties include "Gerdo" (pale pink), "Jaguar" (deep orange-red), "Frisco" (yellow), "Europa" (deep pink), "La Minuette" (cream with pink tips).

SMALL-FLOWERED ROSES. Also known as mini roses. The flowers are less than 3" (8 cm) across and the stem up to 16" (41 cm). There are several popular varieties, including "Disco" (red-pink), "Evelien" (pale pink), "Sabrina" (orange-pink).

SPRAY ROSES. Cultivation of these roses is rapidly expanding. The increased popularity of these cultivars is partly due to their longevity. Just 2 – 2¾" (5 – 7 cm) across, several heads are to be found on each stem. Common varieties include "Evelien" (pink), "Nikita" (red), "Porcelina" (cream), "Alina" (cream-white), "White Princess" (white).

Miniature varieties are also available.

Select roses when the buds are just about to open.

Stems: 14 – 39" (35 – 100 cm).

Special notes: Removing thorns is not advisable, as this leaves gashes in the stem which are prone to bacterial infection. For use in hand-held posies, however, it will be necessary to snip them off. Roses are generally very sensitive to bacteria, which will reduce their cut life, so always use fresh water, clean vases, and flower food. To help prevent infection, remove any foliage below water level.

Never crush the stems. Instead, always make a long, slanted cut.

Frequent misting and a cool environment help to keep both flowers and foliage fresh. If roses wilt, the best way to revive them is by re-cutting the stems under water and standing them in lukewarm water up to their flower heads. Leave them for a couple of hours.

Roses are suitable for home drying, and where florists sell dried flowers they are certainly one of the most commonly available.

Rosa hybrid (spray)

Tall bud vases are the perfect shape for fragrant *Freesia* and spray *Rosa*. A couple of stems of *Freesia* in a vase is an original, alternative gift to a bunch of flowers.

Country-style arrangements are loose and natural, and require garden flowers such as *Calendula*, *Moluccella*, *Physalis* and tiny *Rosa*.

RUDBECKIA
CONEFLOWER, BLACK-EYED SUSAN, GLORIOSA DAISY

R. fulgida, R. hirta, R. nitida; and hybrids.

Rudbeckia nitida

Originating from North America, this bright, daisy-like flower is named after the Swedish botanist Olaus Rudbeck (1630 – 1702). Cultivated from the wild Black-eyed Susan, the flower has been grown in Europe since the seventeenth century.

Season: July – September.
Available in: Yellow, occasionally orange-bronze, purple. Some selections have red-brown centers or prominent green "eyes."
Lasting time: 6 – 8 days.
Flowers: Large, 3 – 5" (8 – 12 cm), and daisy-like, these come in single and double forms. They are also sometimes sold as seed heads, without their petals.
Stems: 24 – 32" (60 – 80 cm).
Special notes: Rudbeckia will wilt extremely quickly if left out of water.

It is advisable to remove stem foliage.

If the flowers start to wilt, re-cut the stems, wrap them tightly in wet paper, and stand in water in a cool, dark place for a few hours.

SAPONARIA
SOAPWORT

S. officinalis, Vaccaria pyramidata (S. vaccaria).

Saponaria is sometimes known as Outdoor Gypsophila, and indeed the pink form of *V. pyramidata* is often grown with white Gypsophila. However, it can be confusing to link the two, for Saponaria has larger flowers and more fleshy stems. Like Gypsophila, however, it is a good filler flower.

Saponaria species

Season: June – September.
Available in: Pink, white.
Lasting time: 6–10 days.
Flowers: *V. pyramidata* has sprays of star-like flowers, each about ½" (1 cm) across. The flowers of *S. officinalis* tend to be larger, at approximately 1 – 1½" (2.5 – 4 cm) across, and hang in terminal clusters. Choose as the flowers are just starting to open.
Stems: 20 – 30" (50 – 70 cm). *V. pyramidata* has slightly shorter cut stems.
Special notes: Saponaria are sensitive to ethylene gas and should be kept away from mature fruit and vegetables, dying flowers, and excess heat.

Scabiosa
Scabious, Pincushion Flower, Sweet Scabious

S. atropurpurea, S. caucasica hybrids, *S. stellata*.

Scabiosa is a plant from the teasel family. From the Latin *scabies*, meaning "the itch," it was thought to be a remedy for the skin disease of that name. *S. caucasica*, the most favored hybrids for florists, originate from the Caucasus and were first cultivated in France, around 1800. The most frequently grown cultivar is "Clive Greaves" (pale blue). *S. stellata* is also known as Drumstick. *Atropurpurea* means "dark crimson," which refers to the original color of the flower and is the predominant color of this more compact-headed, and less common, variety.

Season: June – September/October.
Available in: Scarlet, pink, dark red, red-blue (*S. atropurpurea*); mauve, pale blue, white, with a yellow central disc (*S. caucasica*).
Lasting time: 5 – 10 days.
Flowers: The flowers of *S. caucasica* are large but delicate. Daisy-shaped, each is 2 – 3" (5 – 8

Scabiosa atropurpurea

cm) across, has overlapping petals, and is surrounded by a large central disc with protruding styles. *S. atropurpurea* has rounded double flower heads.
Stems: Erect, slender, almost leafless stems of 10 – 20" (25 – 50 cm), in the case of *S. atropurpurea*. *S. caucasica* are taller, about 20 – 28" (50 – 70 cm).
Special notes: *S. atropurpurea* has a mild, musky scent.

The dried seed heads are excellent for flower arrangements.

Keep these flowers away from excess heat, sunlight, and draughts to ensure maximum longevity. Scabious have weak stems that may need re-cutting to provide good water uptake.

Scabiosa atropurpurea

Scabiosa caucasica

The delicate flower heads of *Aquilegia* are kept apart by *Alchemilla mollis* and protected by several layers of tissue to form a beautiful bouquet.

SCILLA
SQUILL, CUBAN LILY, ENGLISH BLUEBELL, WOOD HYACINTH

S. campanulata (syn. *Endymion hispanicus, Hyacinthoides hispanicus*), *S. peruviana, S. sibirica, S. tubergeniana.*

These flowers resemble wild bluebells, but the cultivated varieties have a greater profusion of florets and are sold without leaves. The May-flowering *S. campanulata* is most often used in mixed spring arrangements.

Season: April – June.
Available in: Blue, some pink, and white
Lasting time: 7 – 10 days.
Flowers: Small and bell-shaped, the flowers of *S. campanulata* are clustered on upright spikes. The Cuban lily (*S. peruviana*), from Algeria and Italy, has dense flower heads, each up to ¾" (19 cm) across, of up to 100 star-shaped, blue flowers. Choose when a few flowers are open but the buds are showing good color.
Stems: Short, thin stems of 8 – 14" (20 – 35 cm). These are reflexed at the tips, until the last flowers open when they gradually straighten. The stems of *S. sibirica* and *S. tubergeniana* are shorter, at 4 – 6" (10 – 15 cm) long.

Scilla species

SEDUM
STONECROP

S. spectabile, S. telephium; and hybrids.

Sedum belongs to the family of succulent plants which includes kalanchoe. The genus originates from eastern Asia and was first cultivated in Great Britain in 1868 and is now grown outdoors all over Europe.

Season: July – October.
Available in: Lavender-pink, cream-orange, various shades of yellow, pink, and white.
Lasting time: Approximately 10 days.
Flowers: Clusters of star-shaped flowers are borne in terminal panicles. Each clustered flower head is 3 – 5" (8 – 13 cm), or more, wide. Choose when most of the florets have opened. If left to mature, flat clusters of seed pods will form.
Stems: 15 – 24" (38 – 61 cm).
Special notes: Remove leaves under water or they will rot and pollute the vase water.

Sedum species

Solidago hybrid

SOLIDAGO
GOLDEN ROD

Solidago hybrids.

From the Latin *soldare,* "to strengthen," this plant is reputed to have medicinal healing properties. Most varieties are available in the summer and autumn, but the cultivar "Super" is available throughout most of the year. Solidago provides a useful filler in arrangements.
Season: July – October.
Available in: Yellow.
Lasting time: 7 – 10 days.
Flowers: Tiny, closely-packed clusters of flowers are formed in feathery, golden, horizontally-spreading sprays. Select where some of the flowers are just starting to open.
Stems: Stiff, branching, tall stems of between 20" and 35" (50 – 89 cm).
Special notes: Suitable for drying.

SOLIDASTER
SOLIDASTER

S. luteus.

Solidaster is a relatively modern hybrid, a cross between Solidago and Aster. It was developed in Lyons in 1909 and it is extensively grown in Europe and Israel. Like Solidago, it is useful as a filler for bouquets.

However, it is less spreading and feathery, having numerous erect, more closely-packed branches.

Season: All year round.
Available in: Yellow.
Lasting time: 8 – 12 days.
Flowers: Tiny flowers appear in loose terminal clusters.
Stems: 24 – 28" (50 – 70 cm).
Special notes: Suitable for drying.

Solidaster luteus

STEPHANOTIS
MADAGASCAR JASMINE,
WAX FLOWER, STEPHANOTIS

S. floribunda.

From the Greek *stephanos*, "a crown" – hence, fit for a crown. This evergreen climbing shrub originates from Madagascar, but has been cultivated in Great Britain since 1839. It is very fragrant, and the short-stemmed waxy flowers are much in demand for bridal work and corsages. Sold in individual clusters or sometimes as single stems.

Season: Most of the year, especially summer.
Available in: White.
Lasting time: A fairly short life of about 4 days.
Flowers: Borne in axillary panicles of up to 8 flowers, each waxy flower consists of a 1½" (4 cm) tubular stem with lobes spreading as much as 2" (5 cm) across.
Stems: 2 – 3" (5 – 8 cm). Sometimes stems are even shorter when sold.
Special notes: Stephanotis flowers are sometimes supplied in inflated bags to protect the petals and maintain a high level of humidity.

Stephanotis floribunda

STRELITZIA
BIRD OF PARADISE FLOWER

S. nicolai, S. reginae.

Strelitzia originate from South America, and these brightly-colored flowers resemble the head of an exotic bird with a brilliant orange crest. They were named after Charlotte of Mecklenburg-Strelitz (1744 – 1818), who

Strelitzia reginae

married King George III to become Queen of England in 1761. The more common species to be found in florists is *S. reginae*.

Season: All year round, with possibly a limited availability in summer.
Available in: Bright orange with blue flowers. The rarer *S. nicolai* has white flowers.
Lasting time: 12 – 18 days.
Flowers: A showy, beaked bract, 6" (15 cm) long, from which emerge a succession of long flowers. The flowers stand erect on each stem to give the appearance of a bird's crest.
Stems: Extremely strong, thick, long, straight stems of 40 – 80" (100 – 200 cm).
Special notes: Purchase Strelitzia when the first flower bud is fully open.

The very large, leathery leaves of this flower are borne on long stalks and provide marvellous foliage for a grand, large-scale design.

Vase life can be prolonged by re-cutting stems. Use secateurs.

Strelitzia oozes jelly-like juices which can make parts of the flower quite sticky and may smell a little unpleasant. Any such juices can be wiped away carefully.

Syringa vulgaris

SYRINGA
LILAC

S. vulgaris.

From the Greek *surinx,* meaning "tube," which apparently alludes to the use of its stems for making reed pipes. Unlike the garden variety, commercially-grown lilac has long, leafless, woody stems, with 2 – 4 flower panicles on each branch. One of the most popular varieties is "Madame Florent Stepman," which is pure white. The mauve and purple varieties have a sweet fragrance. They can be used to make a bold, dramatic arrangement.

Season: October – April (white variety); February – March (mauve/purple varieties).
Available in: White, mauve, purple.
Lasting time: 10 – 15 days. They will last well if treated with cut-flower food.
Flowers: Small, star-shaped, single or double flowers are borne in erect, pyramidal panicles, roughly 6 – 10" (15 – 25 cm) long.
Stems: Straight and leafless. 24 – 39" (60 – 100 cm).
Special notes: Syringa consumes a great deal of water, so vases should be topped up regularly.

Stem ends should be cut off at a very sharp angle using a sharp knife or secateurs. Syringa is often supplied with special flower food.

TRACHELIUM
BLUE THROATWORT

T. caeruleum.

The name is derived from the Greek (*arteria*) *trakheia* meaning "rough artery" or "throat." This plant was used to treat neck and throat disorders. It originates from Portugal and is now cultivated in Europe, particularly Holland.

Season: Although there is limited availability at other times, the main season is April – September.

Available in: Blue, mauve, creamy-white, sometimes pink.

Lasting time: 8 – 12 days.

Flowers: Umbrella-shaped clusters of tiny flowers appear at the top of the stems. Select when they are starting to open.

Stems: Thin stems of 20 – 28" (50 – 70 cm).

Special notes: Trachelium will wilt very quickly if left out of water.

Suitable for drying.

Trachelium caeruleum

TRITELEIA
BRODIAEA

T. laxa.

This is a small lily which originates from California and has been cultivated in Britain since 1888. The variety "Queen Fabiola" was developed in Holland and is the most common variety.

Triteleia laxa

Season: April – July.

Available in: Blue, violet.

Lasting time: 10 – 16 days.

Flowers: Loose, many-flowered, terminal clusters of widely-tubular flowers, each approximately 2" (5 cm) long. Choose where a few flowers in the cluster have opened.

Stems: The flowers are borne on erect, leafless stems of anything from 8 – 20" (20 – 60 cm) long.

Special notes: Removing the lower, white part of the stem will improve longevity.

TULIPA
TULIP

Tulipa hybrids.

Immensely popular as they are all over the world, tulips are native to Turkey, Iran, Syria, and parts of Asia. Their name originates from the Turkish word, *tiilbend*, meaning "turban," which the opened bloom was thought to resemble. They have been cultivated since the sixteenth century and Holland has for many hundreds of years been the main breeder and supplier of new cultivars.

Because tulip stems continue to grow after cutting and because tulips are attracted to the light, their movement will cause change within an arrangement over a period of days. They may look best unmixed and allowed to bend freely. While many people enjoy the curvature of mature tulips, the Dutch like their tulips straight.

Tulipa hybrid (double flowered)

Tulipa hybrid (single flowered)

Season: November – May.
Available in: All colors except blue, and including many two-color varieties.
Lasting time: 5 – 10 days.
Flowers: There is a vast range of tulips, they are divided into early-, mid-, and late-flowering cultivars. There are many sub-categories within these groups, but to simplify, the cut flowers tend to fall into four main groups:
SINGLE TULIPS. These are the most common tulips and have a single row of petals which are usually rounded. These varieties include "Apricot Beauty" (orange-pink), "Atilla" (mauve-pink), and "White Dream" (white).

Tulipa hybrid (lily flowered)

Tulipa hybrid (parrot)

There are also some cultivars with much larger flower heads and stems which can be as long as 39" (100 cm).
DOUBLE TULIPS. These tulips resemble roses or peonies, as they open to reveal several rows of petals. They include "Monte Carlo" (yellow), "Casablanca" (white), and "Angelique" (pink-white).
PARROT TULIPS. These tulips are often two- or three- toned, and this group includes the new fringed varieties. Cultivars include "Rococo" (red and yellow), "Estella Rijnveld" (red, white and green) and "Flaming Parrot" (red and yellow).
LILY-FLOWERED TULIPS. These tulips often have pointed petals and resemble lilies. They include "Aladdin" (red and yellow with white edges), "West Point" (yellow) and "China Pink" (pink).
Tulips may be selected in bud, providing there is good color showing.
Stems: 16 – 39" (40 – 100 cm). Stems will continue to grow in water after cutting, which contributes to their propensity to bend.
Special notes: Tulips are attracted to light and will curve towards it. If this happens, wrap the stems tightly in damp newspaper, secure with an elastic band, and stand in deep, lukewarm water with light directly above them. Leave for a couple of hours.
Ensure tulips have enough water and check the level in the vase frequently.

VALOTTA
SCARBOROUGH LILY

V. speciosa, V. purpurea.

One of the Amaryllis family, and originally from South Africa, these summer flowers have lily-like blooms.

Season: July – October.
Available in: Bright orange-red.
Lasting time: 10 – 14 days.
Flowers: Up to 10 bright, waxy flowers, 3 – 4" (8 – 10 cm) long, are clustered at the top of each stem. Each is open, tunnel-shaped, and

Valotta speciosa

erect. Always choose when one flower is just opening and the other buds show good color.
Stems: A flattened flower stem of 16 – 20" (40 – 50 cm).

VERONICA
SPEEDWELL

V. longifolia, V. virginica, V. spicata hybrids.

V. longifolia originates from Europe and Asia. *V. virginica* originates from Virginia, USA, and has shorter flowers. The elegant flow of the flower racemes makes this an airy addition to arrangements. Veronica is synonymous with Leptandra.

Veronica species

Season: June – September.
Available in: Blue, pale blue; occasionally pink, and white.
Lasting time: 5 – 8 days.
Flowers: Erect flower spikes, at the end of each stem, are approximately 6″ (15 cm) long. They are made up of numerous small florets. Select when some of the lower florets have opened.
Stems: Thin stems of 15 – 24″ (38 – 61 cm).
Special notes: Veronica has a luxuriant growth of glossy stem foliage. Remove two thirds of the leaves before placing in a vase. The flowers will wilt very quickly if left out of water. If wilting does occur, re-cut stems to help with water take-up.

Veronica is sensitive to ethylene gas and should be kept away from mature fruit and vegetables, dying flowers, and excess heat.

VIBURNUM
SNOWBALL TREE, GUELDER ROSE

V. opulus.

Viburnum opulus

Mainly grown in Holland, this shrub has flowers which closely resemble lilac, but are formed in spheres which start green and slowly turn to white. The flowers are fragrant. This is one of the finest all-round shrubs for the flower arranger.

Season: December – March.
Available in: Creamy-white.
Lasting time: 7 – 14 days.
Flowers: Flattish heads, 2 – 4″ (5 – 10 cm) across, are made up of clustered, tubular flowers. Select before the flowers have opened up and the heads as a whole still appear light green.
Stems: Branched, woody stems, from 20 – 30″ (50 – 76 cm).
Special notes: Viburnum will wilt very quickly if left out of water. When cutting the stem, make a clean diagonal cut using a sharp knife or secateurs.

Always use recommended cut-flower food in the vase water.

VIOLA
SWEET VIOLET

V. cornula hybrids, *V. odorata.*

Related to the pansy family, violets have been cultivated for centuries, particularly in southern France for the perfume industry. Violets are usually sold in tiny bunches surrounded by their leaves, and they have a sweet fragrance.

Season: February – May.
Available in: Mid- to deep-violet, and sometimes in white.
Lasting time: 3 – 6 days.
Flowers: Showy, single, pansy-like flowers, ¾″ (2 cm) across, come in single and double forms. Choose when the flowers are starting to open.
Stems: Short. 4 – 6″ (10 – 15 cm).
Special notes: Avoid excess heat and direct sunlight. On the other hand, too cold an atmosphere will reduce their fragrance.

ments and to some extent in funeral arrangements – although they are also popular bridal flowers, signifying purity. *Z. aethiopica* is the variety known commonly as the Calla lily.

Zantedeschia species

Season: All year round. The peak period for white varieties is February – May, and for colored varieties, June – August.
Available in: White, cream, yellow, pink, green.
Lasting time: 10 -14 days.
Flowers: Single flowers are borne on a spadix at the end of the stem. The length of the spathe will vary with the variety, and can be from 3 – 5" (8 – 12 cm) in length. They should be selected when they are completely open and erect.
Stems: A long, straight stem of 15 – 39" (38 – 100 cm). *Z. aethiopica* is the largest species, with stems about 36" long, while others may be under 24" (60 cm).
Special notes: These flowers prefer a cool atmosphere.

Zantedeschia take in a lot of water, so check vase water levels regularly.

Viola odorata

> # ZANTEDESCHIA
> CALLA LILY, ARUM LILY

Z. aethiopica, Z. albo-maculata, Z. elliottiana, Z. rehmannii; and hybrids.

There are various varieties of these striking lilies which originate from Africa and are now grown in Europe. The white varieties have traditionally been used in church arrange-

> # ZINNIA
> YOUTH AND OLD AGE

Z. elegans hybrids.

Originating from Mexico and first cultivated in Austria in 1613, Zinnia are a popular garden

Scabious and *Lathyrus* are relatively short-lived summer flowers, but their longevity will be increased if they are kept in a very cool, shady environment.

flower, as well as being widely commercially cultivated, particularly in the USA. The flower heads vary in shape, but resemble Dahlias. Suited to both traditional and modern designs, they will add a highlight to an arrangement.

Season: May – October.
Available in: Virtually every color except blue – bright shades of red, orange, yellow, pink, salmon, white, and mauve.
Lasting time: 6 – 10 days.
Flowers: Multi-petalled round forms of approximately 2" (5 cm) in diameter, with a single head on each stem. Some forms are button type while others are much looser.
Stems: Rough, erect stems, which sometimes kink just below the flower head. 20 – 24" (50 – 60 cm) and longer. Some smaller kinds are also available on short, 6 – 8" (15 – 20 cm) stems.
Special notes: A small length of wire, inserted through the top of the flowers down into the stem, will correct any kink that forms (see above), without any harmful effect on their cut life.

Zinnia elegans

CUT FOLIAGE

ANTHURIUM
ANTHURIUM

A. andreanum, A. crystallinum, A. scherzerianum.

Ornamental leaves which accompany the cut flower. These shiny heart-shaped leaves vary in size and shape.

A. andreanum is the most commonly used species for foliage. Its leaves are up to 8" (20 cm) long. *A. crystallinum* has velvety leaves up to 24" (61 cm) long and 12" (30 cm) across. *A. scherzerianum* has leaves up to 7" (18 cm) long. Because the leaves are often damaged on the plant, these leaves are not necessarily easy to obtain. Misting the leaves regularly will keep them in optimum condition.

Season: All year round.
Available in: Dark green (*A. andreanum* and. *A. scherzerianum*) *A. crystallinum* are violet when young, maturing to deep green, with midribs and veins in ivory, above, and pale pink, beneath.
Lasting time: 10 – 18 days.
Stems: 20 – 28" (50 – 70 cm).

Anthurium species

Asparagus asparagoides medeoloides

ASPARAGUS

Cultivars of *A. asparagoides, A. densiflorus, A. setaceus, A. pyramidalis.*

A wide variety of small-leaved, needled and feathery Asparagus ferns are available (see below). Frequent misting with water will help prevent needles of all these varieties from drying up, and will therefore help to avoid premature leaf drop.

SMILAX, GREENBRIER
....
A. asparagoides/A. asparagoides medeoloides.

Smilax (*A. asparagoides medeoloides*) has smaller, oval, lighter green leaves than the other Asparagus varieties. It can be found in two forms: one especially cultivated in twining stems, often with several strands wired together; and the other cut from the wild.

Season: May be limited to spring and summer months.

Available in: Bright green.

Lasting time: Smilax has a shorter cut life than other Asparagus varieties, at between a week and 10 days.

Stems: Long, thin, wiry, trailing stems of 36 – 48″ (91 – 122 cm).

MING FERN
....

A. densiflorus/A. densiflorus myriocladus.

This is a branched and heavily tufted type. It tends to be sold in smaller bunches than the other varieties.

Season: All year round.

Available in: Green.

Lasting time: An especially long-lasting variety of Asparagus, 20 – 28 days.

Stems: 16 – 39″ (40 – 100 cm).

Asparagus densiflorus myriocladus

SPRENGER FERN, SPRENGERI, (TREE FERN)
....

A. densiflorus/A. densiflorus sprengeri.

Dark-green, needle-like leaves and tiny thorns are set closely together. *A. pyramidalis* (the tree fern) is similar to the Sprenger fern.

Asparagus densiflorus sprengeri

Asparagus setaceus plumosus

Season: All year round.
Available in: Green.
Lasting time: 14 – 20 days.
Stems: 16 – 39" (40 – 100 cm).

ASPARAGUS FERN, LACY FERN, PLUMOSA
....
A. setaceus/A. setaceus plumosus.

This is a feathery variety, which comes in dark and light shades. Typically, Asparagus fern is sold by the bunch.

Season: All year round.
Available in: Green.
Lasting time: 14 – 20 days.
Stems: Trailing or erect, 16 – 39" (40 – 100 cm).

ASPIDISTRA
CAST IRON PLANT

A. elatior.

Its common name indicates the tough resilience of the long leaves – up to 20" (50 cm) long – which can be washed and treated to give a more shiny appearance. Aspidistra is

Aspidistra elatior

commonly grown as a house plant, because it is so tolerant to changes in temperature, gas fumes, and poor light.

Season: All year round.
Available in: Deep green and variegated with cream stripes.
Lasting time: 14 – 21 days.
Stems: 20 – 28" (50 – 70 cm).

BUXUS

B. sempervirens (English box), *B. microphylla japonica* and *B. microphylla koreana* cultivars.

BOX, ENGLISH / KOREAN / JAPANESE BOXWOOD
....
Box leaves are small, oblong to ovate, and on woody branches. Typically Box is sold in bundles. When the leaves of *B. sempervirens* are crushed they have a peppery fragrance.

Season: All year round.
Available in: Glossy, dark green; some variegated white and variegated yellow varieties.
Lasting time: 10 – 14 days.
Stems: Woody, 20 – 28" (50 – 70 cm).

Buxus sempervirens

OREGONIA
....

B. sempervirens – variegated varieties.

A variegated variety of Box, Oregonia is to be found sold in bundles of branches.

Season: All year round, but less common in summer.
Available in: Green, variegated with white. Small, blue-black fruits appear on mature shrubs.
Lasting time: 10 – 14 days.
Stems: Woody, 20 – 28″ (50 – 70 cm).

CODIAEUM
CROTON

C. variegatum pictum, and cultivars.

These variegated leaves are available in various shapes – ranging from linear to ovate – and various sizes and colors. They can be obtained both as whole stems and as single leaves.

Buxus sempervirens (variegated)

Season: All year round.
Available in: Multi-colored combinations ranging from pink, red, orange, and almost black, to green with yellow or white spots or blotches.
Lasting time: 7 days.
Stems: From pot-plant height of about 12″ (30 cm), to vigorous plants from 48″ (122 cm), to as much as 120″ (305 cm).

Codiaeum variegatum pictum

CYCAS
PALM, SAGO PALM

C. revoluta.

These palm leaves, borne on a straight stem, are quite stiff. Combined with a flower such as Proteas, they can create a dramatic graphic arrangement. When dry, they turn a light, creamy-brown color.

Cycas revoluta

Season: All year round.
Available in: Dark green.
Lasting time: 21 – 28 days.
Stems: 20 – 28″ (50 – 70 cm).

CYPERUS
UMBRELLA GRASS, PALM CROWN

C. alternifolius.

Cyperus is a moisture-loving plant with "umbrellas" – spanning 6 – 12″ (15 – 30 cm) – of thin, arching, leaf-like bracts, at the end of a clump of long, stiff, bare, dark-green stems. *C. alternifolius* is usually grown as a pot plant. Misting leaves will encourage longevity.

Season: All year round.
Available in: Green.
Lasting time: 21 – 28 days.
Stems: 28 – 39″ (70 – 100 cm).

PAPYRUS

C. papyrus.

Short, stiff, grass-like, inflorescences appear at the top of tall, thick, smooth, dark green stems, to form globulous heads of approximately 12″ (30 cm) across.

Season: All year round.
Available in: Green.
Lasting time: 21 – 28 days.
Stems: 28 – 39″ (70 – 100 cm).

Cyperus alternifolius

Cyperus papyrus

Eucalyptus species (oval leaved)

EUCALYPTUS
GUM TREE, SILVER DOLLAR,
MALLEE, EUCALYPTUS

E. cinerea, E. nicolli, E. parvifolia, E. perriniana,
E. populus, E. pulverulenta, E. tetragona.

There are many varieties of Eucalyptus. Some
have oval leaves (*E. populus* and *E. stuartina*),
some long (*E. parvifolia* and *E. nicolli*), others
round – and sometimes double – such as *E.
cinerea* (silver dollar) and *E. gunnii*. *E. perriniana* (round-leaved snow gum or spinning
gum) has leaves, when young, of a beautiful
lavender color.

For flowers such as Irises, which can look
their best when displayed unmixed with other
flowers, Eucalyptus is a superb foliage addition for creating a fuller but cohesive arrangement. Seed pods are also available. Eucalyptus
is typically sold in bunches. Eucalyptus has a
strong menthol aroma.

Eucalyptus species (round leaved)

Season: All year round, although less common in summer.
Available in: Green, silver-green, blue-green. Many of the species are found dyed in a range of colors for dried arrangements.
Lasting time: 10 – 14 days.
Stems: 20 – 39" (50 – 100 cm).

EUONYMUS
SPINDLE

E. japonicus, E. fortunei.

Leathery, shiny, oval leaves which grow close together on very tough stems. "Silver Queen" has white variegated leaves. "Yellow Queen" has yellow variegated leaves.

Season: All year round.
Available in: Green, variegated white, variegated yellow.
Lasting time: 14 – 21 days.
Stems: 20 – 24" (50 – 60 cm).

Eucalyptus species (round leaved)

Eucalyptus species (long leaved)

Euonymus species (variegated)

Summer is the time for celebrating blue flowers. Deep blue *Delphinium* and *Centaurea cyanus* mix beautifully with purple-tinged *Alstroemeria* and grey-green *Eucalyptus*.

Yellow *Leucadendron*, *Protea* and spiky *Cynara scolymus* (globe artichoke) heads are combined with the trailing stems of *Bupleurum* to create a modern, rustic foliage arrangement for winter.

Hedera helix

HEDERA
IVY

H. helix, H. canariensis, H. colchica.

Trails of ivy are often sold with their roots. They have curly, pointed, or heart-shaped leaves. *H. helix,* or English ivy, is the most popular ivy. *H. canariensis* is known as Algerian ivy, and *H. colchica* as Persian ivy. Sometimes sold in bunches, whole plants are usually more suitable to use for corsages or bridal work. Frequent misting with water is recommended.

Season: All year round.
Available in: Green, variegated white, variegated yellow.
Lasting time: Up to 7 days.
Stems: 20 – 39" (50 – 100 cm).

ILEX
HOLLY

I. aquifolium.

These glossy, dark-green leaves with sharp spines are, of course, much used for Christmas decoration.

Ilex aquifolium

Season: November and December.
Available in: Green, or variegated in green and yellow/green and white. Bearing red berries.
Lasting time: 10 – 16 days.
Stems: Usually long, the lengths available from florists vary considerably.

MYRTUS
MYRTLE

M. communis.

There are two main types of Myrtus available, a tall variety of up to 48" (120 cm), with large, glossy, green leaves; and a shorter 12" (30 cm) variety with smaller leaves. The variegated variety has white-edged leaves.

Myrtle leaves have a pleasant, spicy scent when crushed. Typically myrtle is sold in branches, but it can also be grown as an evergreen pot plant.

Season: All year round, but particularly in winter and early spring.
Available in: Green. The variegated variety has white-edged leaves.
Lasting time: 5 – 10 days.
Stems: 12 – 48" (30 – 128 cm).

Myrtus communis

NEPHROLEPIS
SHARON FERN

Nephrolepis species.

A wide variety of sword-shaped ferns which vary in shape, length, and color.

Frequent misting will help to keep the fronds fresh.

Season: All year round.
Available in: Green.
Lasting time: 10 – 14 days.
Stems: 12 – 24" (30 – 60 cm).

SWORD FERN, BOSTON FERN
....

N. exaltata "Bostoniensis".

This has short, pale green leaves on stems of up to 30" (76 cm). It should be noted that the name "sword fern" is also used to refer to a foliage called Polystichum.

Nephrolepis species

OREGON FERN, FLAT FERN, BRAKE
FERN, LADDER FERN

....

N. exaltata cordifolia.

This fern is darker green and longer than
Boston fern. The common name "brake fern"
is also used to refer to *Rumohra adiantiformus*
(African leatherleaf fern).

PITTOSPORUM
AUSTRALIAN LAUREL, MOCK ORANGE, PITT

P. tobira.

A shrubby foliage with leathery leaves and
very tough stems, grown as an evergreen
hedge or house plant. Clusters of small yellow
flowers grow in the summer. It is typically
sold in bundles or branches.

Season: All year round.
Available in: Medium- to light-green, varie-
gated white, variegated yellow/cream.
Lasting time: 10 – 18 days.
Stems: 12 – 24" (30 – 60 cm).

Pittosporum tobira

Rumohra adiantiformis

RUMOHRA
LEATHER FERN

R. adiantiformis.

R. adiantiformis is the most popular leatherleaf-
type fern available. It is also known as African
fern or brake fern or elephant fern. Grown in
Central America for export, this extremely
tough fern withstands transportation well. It
is similar to *Arachniodes adiantiformus* and
Dryopteris erythrosora (Buckler fern or
American leatherleaf), which have stiff, dark,
glossy leaves. *R. adiantiformis* has larger, wider
fronds, but is paler and less stiff than the
American leatherleaf. It is normally sold in
bunches.

When choosing leatherleaf, roll the end of a
frond between your fingers. If it is not stiff
enough to roll, it is not ideal and will turn
brown early. Misting is recommended. Re-cut
stems and change vase water frequently.

Season: All year round.
Available in: Green.
Lasting time: 14 – 21days.
Stems: 20 – 24" (50 – 60 cm).

RUSCUS
BUTCHER'S BROOM, BOX HOLLY

R. aculeatus, R. hypoglossum, R. racemosus.

There are several varieties of Ruscus with glossy, oval leaves. *R. aculeatus* has smaller, more pointed leaves than *R. hypoglossum*. Ruscus is usually sold in bunches.

Season: All year round, but less common in summer.
Available in: Dark green.
Lasting time: 10 – 14 days.
Stems: Straight stems of 16 – 35" (40 – 90 cm).

Ruscus hypoglossum

Ruscus aculeatus

Ruscus racemosus

ALEXANDRIAN LAUREL, SOFT RUSCUS
....

R. racemosus (Syn. *Danae racemosa*).

This variety of Ruscus is one of the most popular foliages with flower arrangers. It has long, pointed, dark-green, shiny leaves. In fact, as in other species of Ruscus, they are not leaves at all, but flattened shoots with a leaf-like appearance – each approximately 4 – 10" (10 – 25cm) long.

Season: All year round, and often producing inconspicuous, sulphur-yellow flowers in early summer, and round, orange-red berries in fall.
Available in: Dark green.
Lasting time: 10 – 14 days.
Stems: These are shiny, pliable, and arching, and resemble leaves. Approximately 12 – 40" (30 – 101 cm).

XEROPHYLLUM
BEAR GRASS

X. tenax, D. texanum.

Also known as Dasylirion, this grass is up to 36" (91 cm) in length. These long, thin leaves have become very popular in contemporary arrangements. Bear grass is usually available in bunches. Suitable for drying.

Season: All year round.
Available in: Green.
Lasting time: 10 – 20 days.
Stems: Available as short and long stems. The short lengths are up to 30" (76 cm) but they can be much longer.

Xerophyllum tenax

APPENDIX

BIRTHDAY FLOWERS

There are flowers and foliage designated to represent every sign of the zodiac. With some exceptions, the flowers are in season during these months.

Colors associated with star signs may also suggest suitable flowers for making an original birthday - present bouquet (see colored flowers, page 180).

AQUARIUS
(January 20 – February 18)
COLORS: *Electric blue, turquoise*
Gardenia
Hydrangea
Orchidaceae
Tulipa

PISCES
(February 19 – March 20)
COLORS: *Soft green, silvery white*
Lilium, white
Narcissus (Daffodil)
Orchidaceae, white
Zinnia

ARIES
(March 21 – April 19)
COLOR: *Red*
Carthamus
Dianthus, red
Muscari
Rosa, red

TAURUS
(April 20 – May 20)
COLORS: *Pink, pale blue, pale green, emerald green*
Acacia
Papaver
Rosa, pink
Syringa

GEMINI
(May 21 – June 20)
COLOR: *Yellow*
Convallaria
Lathyrus
Lilium
Polianthes tuberosa

CANCER
(June 21 – July 22)
COLORS: *Smoky gray, silvery blue, iridescent blue*
Ammi
Iris
Rosa, white
Zantedeschia

LEO
(July 23 – August 22)
COLORS: *Orange, golden yellow*
Calendula
Helianthus
Paeonia
Palm

VIRGO
(August 23 – September 22)
COLORS: *Navy blue, dark brown, green, violet*
Centaurea cyanus
Matthiola
Phlox
Veronica

LIBRA
(September 23 – October 22)
COLORS: *Pale pink, pale blue, pale green, harmonious greens*
Gentiana
Hydrangea
Lupinus
Rosa, large headed

SCORPIO
(October 23 – November 21)
COLORS: *Deep red, maroon, scarlet*
Althaea
Buxus
Chrysanthemum, red
Lilium, red

SAGITTARIUS
(November 22 – December 21)
COLORS: *Rich purple, dark blue, red, royal blue*
Echinops
Dianthus
Dianthus barbatus
Solidago

CAPRICORN
(December 22 – January 19)
COLORS: *Dark green, gray, black, brown, indigo*
Centaurea cyanus
Galanthus
Hedera
Myosotis

SCENTED FLOWERS

All of the following flowers have a distinctive and pleasant perfume:

Acacia dealbata	Sharp citrus fragrance	
Anetheum	Strongly aromatic scent of dill	
Bouvardia longiflora	Sweetly scented	
Chamelaucium	Both leaves and flowers are scented	
Chrysanthemum parthenium	Peppery fragrance similar to camomile	
Convallaria	Heavy, sweet scent	
Dianthus plumarius	Spicy fragrance	
Eucharis	Soft scent	
Freesia	The red varieties tend to have most perfume	
Gardenia	Heavy, exotic perfume	
Genista	Light, sweet fragrance	
Hyacinthus	Heavy, sweet perfume	
Lathyrus	Very heavy, sweet fragrance	
Lavandula	Distinctive stong scent	
Lilium	Particularly longiflorum, and oriental hybrids –	

"Casablanca" (white), "Stargazer" (striped pink), "Furore" (white)

Matthiola	Heavy, peppery fragrance
Narcissus	Particularly jonquil, polyanthus, and tazetta varieties
Phlox	Sweet scent
Polianthes	Very heavy, sweet fragrance
Rose	Some varieties, including "Jacaranda" (pink), "Osiana" (peach),"Baccara" (red), "Madame Delbard" (red), "Jack Frost" (green-white), "Sterling Silver" (silver-pink)
Stephanotis	Sweet, heavy perfume
Syringa	Lilac and purple varieties
Viburnum	Sweet-scented
Viola	Faint, sweet scent

Lilium longiflorum

Freesia hybrids

SEASONAL FLOWER AVAILABILITY

FLOWERS AVAILABLE ALL YEAR ROUND

Ageratum	Aster ericoides	Dendrobium	Hippeastrum	Oncidium
Alpinia	Atriplex	Dianthus	Iris	Ornithogalum
Alstroemeria	Banksia	Euphorbia	Leucadendron	Paphiopedilum
Ananas	Bouvardia	marginata	Leucospermum	Phalaenopsis
Anethum	Bupleurum	Freesia	Liatris	Protea
Anigozanthos	Calendula	Gardenia	Lilium	Rosa
Anthurium	Chrysanthemum	Gerbera	Limonium	Solidaster
Antirrhinum	Cirsium	Gladiolus	Matthiola	Stephanotis
Arachnis	Cymbidium	Gypsophila	Moluccella	Strelitzia
Aranthera	Delphinium	Heliconia	Nerine	Zantedeschia

FLOWERS AVAILABLE IN WINTER

Acacia	Banksia	Delphinium	Hyacinthus	Prunus
Agapanthus	Chamaelaucium	Euphorbia fulgens	Lilium	Strelitzia
Ammi	Chrysanthemum	Galanthus	Muscari	Syringa
Anemone	parthenium	Helleborus	Narcissus	Tulipa

FLOWERS AVAILABLE IN AUTUMN

Acacia	Aster novi-belgii	Echinops	Hypericum	Physostegia
Achillea	Callistephus	Euphorbia fulgens	Kniphofia	Rudbeckia
Aconitum	Celosia	Eustoma	Lathyrus	Saponaria
Agapanthus	Chrysanthemum	Freesia	Lavandula	Scabiosa
Allium	parthenium	Gloriosa	Lavatera	Sedum
Amaranthus	Coreopsis	Gomphrena	Matthiola	Solidago
Anemone	Cosmos	Helianthus	Montbretia	Tulipa
Antirrhinum	Craspedia	Helichrysum	Nerine	Valotta
Aquilegia	Dahlia	Hydrangea	Phlox	Zinnia

Euphorbia fulgens

Scabiosa caucasica

FLOWERS AVAILABLE IN SUMMER

Achillea
Aconitum
Agapanthus
Alchemilla
Allium
Althaea
Amaranthus
Anemone
Aquilegia
Asclepias
Astilbe
Astrantia
Bouvardia
Callistephus
Campanula

Carthamus
Celosia
Centaurea
Chrysanthemum
  frutescens
Coreopsis
Cosmos
Craspedia
Crocosmia
Dahlia
Delphinium
  consolida
Dianthus barbatus
Digitalis
Dimorpotheca

Doronicum
Echinops
Eremurus
Erigeron
Eryngium
Eucharis
Eustoma
Gentiana
Gloriosa
Godetia
Gomphrena
Helenium
Helianthus
Helichrysum
Hydrangea

Hypericum
Ixia
Kniphofia
Lathyrus
Lavandula
Lavatera
Lilium
Lupinus
Lysimachia
Myosotis
Nigella
Paeonia
Papaver
Phlox
Physostegia

Polianthes
  tuberosa
Rudbeckia
Sandersonia
Saponaria
Scabiosa
Scilla
Sedum
Solidago
Trachelium
Triteleia
Valotta
Veronica
Vibernum
Zinnia

FLOWERS AVAILABLE IN SPRING

Acacia
Alchemilla
Allium
Ammi
Anemone
Aquilegia
Campanula

Centaurea
Chamaelaucium
Convallaria
Craspedia
Dianthus barbatus
Doronicum
Eremurus

Erigeron
Eustoma
Freesia
Genista
Gloriosa
Godetia
Helianthus

Helleborus
Hyacinthus
Ixia
Lathyrus
Muscari
Narcissus
Prunus

Ranunculus
Scilla
Syringa
Triteleia
Tulipa
Viburnum
Viola

Lathyrus odoratus

Muscari species

COLORED FLOWERS

The following flowers are categorized according to their most commonly available colors. Cultivars of the genus may well be available in additional colors, and these will be indicated in the main flower entries. Certain flowers are also to be found dyed, in a range of hues.

YELLOW

Acacia	Cattleya	Digitalis	Helichrysum	Oncidium
Achillea	Celosia	Dimorphotheca	Heliconia	Papaver
Alchemilla mollis	Centaurea	Doronicum	Hippeastrum	Paphiopedilum
Alpinia	macrocephala	Eremerus	Hypericum	Phalaenopsis
Alstroemeria	Chrysanthemum	Erigeron	Iris	Protea
Anethum	Coreopsis	Euphorbia fulgens	Kniphofia	Ranunculus
Anigozanthos	Cosmos	Freesia	Leucadendron	Rosa
Antirrhinum	Craspedia	Genisia	Leucospermum	Rudbeckia
Aqueligia	Crocosmia	Gerbera	Lilium	Solidago
Arachnis	Cymbidium	Gladiolus	Lupinus	Solidaster
Banksia	Dahlia	Gloriosa	Mahonia	Tulipa
Calendula	Dendrobium	Helenium	Matthiola	Zantedeschia
Callistephus	Dianthus	Helianthus	Narcissus	Zinnia

ORANGE

Alstroemeria	Chrysanthemum	Euphorbia fulgens	Ixia	Protea
Antirrhinum	Coreopsis	Freesia	Kniphofia	Ranunculus
Aranthera	Cosmos	Gerbera	Lathyrus	Rosa
Asclepias	Crocosmia	Gladiolus	Leucadendron	Rudbeckia
Banksia	Cymbidium	Godetia	Leucospermum	Sandersonia
Calendula	Dahlia	Gomphrena	Lilium	Strelitzia
Carthamus	Dianthus	Helichrysum	Papaver	Tritonia
Cattleya	Dimorphotheca	Heliconia	Phalaenopsis	Tulipa
Celosia	Eremurus	Hippeastrum	Physalis	Zinnia

Tulipa hybrid

Calendula officinalis

RED

Achillea	Aranthera	Cymbidium	Helenium	Matthiola
Allium	Aster	Dahlia	Helichrysum	Nerine
Alpinia	Astilbe	Dendrobium	Heliconia	Papaver
Alstroemeria	Atriplex	Dianthus	Hippeastrum	Paphiopedilum
Amaranthus	Bouvardia	Freesia	Ixia	Protea
Anemone	Callistephus	Genista	Kniphofia	Ranunculus
Anigozanthos	Celosia	Gerbera	Lathyrus	Rosa
Anthurium	Chamaelaucium	Gladiolus	Leucadendron	Scabiosa
Antirrhinum	Cirsium	Gloriosa	Leucospermum	Tulipa
Aquilegia	Cosmos	Godetia	Lilium	Valotta
Arachnia	Crocosmia	Gomphrena	Lupinus	Zinnia

PINK

Achillea	Campanula	Eremurus	Ixia	Odontoglossum
Allium	Cattleya	Erigeron	Kniphofia	Paeonia
Alpinia	Centaurea	Euphorbia fulgens	Lathyrus	Paphiopedilum
Althaea	Chamelaucium	Eustoma	Lavandula	Phalaenopsis
Alstroemeria	Chrysanthemum	Freesia	Lavatera	Phlox
Ananas	Cirsium	Gerbera	Leucadendron	Protea
Anemone	Cosmos	Gladiolus	Leucospermum	Prunus
Anthurium	Cymbidium	Godetia	Liatris	Ranunculus
Antirrhinum	Dahlia	Gomphrena	Lilium	Rosa
Aquilegia	Delphinium	Gypsophila	Limonium	Saponaria
Aster	consolida	Helichrysum	Lisianthus	Scilla
Astilbe	Dendrobium	Heliconia	Lupinus	Trachelium
Astrantia	Dianthus	Hippeastrum	Matthiola	Tulipa
Bouvardia	Digitalis	Hyacinthus	Nerine	Verbena
Callistephus	Dimorphotheca	Hydrangea	Nigella	Zantedeschia

Ixia species

Gerbera jamesonii

Purple

Achillea
Aconitum
Ageratum
Allium
Alpinia
Alstroemeria
Anemone
Antirrhinum
Aquilegia
Aster
Astrantia

Callistephus
Campanula
Cattleya
Cirsium
Cosmos
Dahlia
Delphinium
Dendrobium
Dianthus
Erigeron
Eustoma

Freesia
Gerbera
Gladiolus
Godetia
Gomphrena
Helichrysum
Heliconia
Helleborus
Hippeastrum
Iris
Ixia

Lathyrus
Liatris
Limonium
Lisianthus
Lupinus
Matthiola
Muscari
Nigella
Phalaenopsis
Phlox
Physostegia

Protea
Rosa
Rudbeckia
Scabiosa
Scilla
Syringa
Trachelium
Triteleia
Tulipa
Veronica
Zinnia

Blue

Aconitum
Agapanthus
Ageratum
Allium
Aquilegia
Brodiaea

Callistephus
Campanula
Centaurea
Delphinium
Echinops
Erigeron

Eryngium
Gentiana
Hyacinthus
Hydrangea
Iris
Lavandula

Limonium
Lisianthus
Mahonia
Muscari
Myosotis
Nigella

Scabiosa
Scilla
Trachelium
Triteleia
Veronica
Viola

Green

Alchemilla
  mollis

Amaranthus
Ananas

Anethum
Bupleurum

Euphorbia
  marginata

Helichrysum
Moluccella

Allium giganteum

Centaurea cyanus

WHITE

Achillea
Agapanthus
Ageratum
Allium
Alstroemeria
Ammi
Anemone
Anthurium
Antirrhinum
Aquilegia
Aster
Astilbe
Astrantia
Bouvardia
Callistephus
Campanula
Cattleya

Chamaelaucium
Chrysanthemum
    frutescens
Convallaria
Cosmos
Cymbidium
Dahlia
Delphinium
Dendrobium
Dianthus
Digitalis
Dimorphotheca
Eremurus
Erigeron
Eucharis
Euphorbia fulgens
Eustoma

Freesia
Galanthus
Gardenia
Genista
Gentiana
Gerbera
Gladiolus
Gomphrena
Gypsophila
Helianthus
Helichrysum
Helleborus
Hippeastrum
Hyacinthus
Hydrangea
Iris
Ixia

Kniphofia
Lathyrus
Lilium
Limonium
Lisianthus
Lupinus
Lysimachia
Matthiola
Narcissus
Nigella
Odontoglossum
Ornithogalum
Paeonia
Paphiopedilum
Phalaenopsis
Phlox
Physostegia

Polianthes
    tuberosa
Protea
Prunus
Ranunculus
Rosa
Saponaria
Scabiosa
Scilla
Stephanotis
Syringa
Tulipa
Veronica
Viburnum
Viola
Zantedeschia
Zinnia

MIXED COLORS

Allium
Alstroemeria
Anemone
Anigozanthos
Aquilegia
Arachnis
Aster
Callistephus

Chrysanthemum
Cymbidium
Dianthus
Digitalis
Eremurus
Erigeron
Eustoma
Freesia

Gerbera
Gloriosa
Helichrysum
Hippeastrum
Iris
Kniphofia
Lathyrus
Lilium

Limonium
Lupinus
Lisianthus
Matthiola
Myosotis
Nerine
Papaver
Phlox

Protea
Ranunculus
Rosa
Scabiosa
Strelitzia
Tulipa
Zantedeschia
Zinnia

Eucharis grandiflora

Kniphofia uvaria

FLOWERS FOR LARGE AND SMALL ARRANGEMENTS

LONG-STEMMED FLOWERS

Aconitum
Agapanthus
Allium giganteum
Alpina purpurata
Alstroemeria
Althaea
Ammi

Anethum
Anigozanthos
Antirrhinum
Aster
Atriplex
Cirsium
Delphinium

Delphinium
  consolida
Digitalis
Eremurus
Euphorbia fulgens
Gerbera
Gladiolus

Helianthus
Heliconia
Lilium
Lupinus
Moluccella
Phalaenopsis
Polianthes tuberosa

Prunus
Rudbeckia
Solidago
Solidaster
Strelitzia
Syringa
Zantedeschia

SHORT-STEMMED FLOWERS

Convallaria
Galanthus
Gardenia

Gladioli (mini)
Gloriosa
Helleborous

Hyacinthus
Iris (mini)
Muscari

Oncidium (mini)
Paphiopedilum
Protea

Scabiosa purpurata
Stephanotis
Viola

FLOWERS WITH LARGE FLOWERS OR FLOWER HEADS

Achillea
  filipendulina
Allium giganteum
Banksia
Cattleya
Chrysanthemum
  blooms

Cymbidium
Dahlia
Dianthus
  caryophyllus/
  barbatus
Eremurus
Gerbera

Gloriosa
Helianthus
Heliconia
Hippeastrum
Hyacinthus
Hydrangea
Kniphofia

Lavatera
Leucospermum
Lilium
Mahonia
Matthiola
Paeonia
Phalaenopsis

Protea
Rosa
  (large-headed)
Sedum
Strelitzia
Syringa
Zantedeschia

Stephanotis floribunda

Strelitzia reginae

LONG-LASTING FLOWERS

Provided these flowers are bought in early maturity and are kept in fresh water, in clean vases with flower food added, they should last two weeks, and possibly longer.

Achillea filipedulina	Banksia	Eryngium	Heliconia	Paphiopedilum
Agapanthus	Bouvardia	Echinops	Leucadendron	Protea
Allium	Chrysanthemum	Eustoma	Lilium	Strelitzia
Alpinia purpurata	Dendrobium	Gentiana	Limonium	Syringa
Alstroemeria	Dianthus	Gladiolus	Mahonia	Triteleia
Anthurium	caryophyllus	Helichrysum	Ornithogalum	

FLOWERS SUITABLE FOR DRYING

Acacia	(Air)	Chamaelaucium	(Air)	Leucadendron	(Air)
Achillea	(Air/ Microwave)	Cirsium	(Air)	Liatris	(Air)
		Chrysanthemum	(Air/Desiccant /Microwave)	Limonium	(Air)
Aconitum	(Air)			Moluccella	(Air)
Agapanthus	(Desiccant)	Convallaria	(Desiccant)	Muscari	(Desiccant)
Ageratum	(Air)	Cosmea	(Desiccant)	Nigella	(Air)
Alchemilla	(Air)	Craspedia	(Air)	Orchidaceae	(Microwave)
Allium	(Air)	Delphinium consolida	(Air/ Desiccant)	Paeonia	(Air/ Microwave)
Amaranthus	(Air)				
Ananas	(Air)	Dianthus	(Desiccant/ Microwave)	Papaver	(Desiccant)
Anemone	(Microwave/ Desiccant)			Physalis	(Air)
		Euchinops	(Air)	Protea	(Air)
Antirrhinum	(Desiccant)	Eryngium	(Air/ Desiccant)	Ranunculus	(Air)
Anigozanthos	(Air)			Rosa	(Air/ Desiccant/ Microwave)
Astilbe	(Air)	Freesia	(Desiccant)		
Astrantia	(Air)	Gomphrena	(Air)		
Atriplex	(Air)	Gypsophila	(Air/ Microwave)	Scabiosa	(Air)
Banksia	(Air)			Sedum	(Microwave)
Calendula	(Desiccant)	Helichrysum	(Air)	Solidago	(Air)
Carthamus	(Air)	Hydrangea	(Air/ Microwave)	Solidaster	(Air)
Celosia	(Air)			Trachelium	(Air)
Centaurea	(Air/Desiccant/ Microwave)	Lavandula	(Air)	Tulipa	(Microwave)
		Leptospermum	(Air)	Zinnia	(Desiccant)

Banksia species   *Zinnia elegans*

Tall *Gerbera* need the support of a high vase, and the crinkled edges keep the stems apart. Here they are interspersed with tied bunches of *Xerophyllum*.

INDEX OF COMMON NAMES

Page numbers in italics indicate photographs of flower arrangements.

BIBLIOGRAPHY

VAUGHAN, Mary Jane, *The Complete Book of Cut Flower Care*, Timber Press, 9999 S W Wilshire, Portland, Oregon 97225, USA; 1988.

GELEIN, Coen and JOORE, Nees, *Decorative Cut Flowers*, Cassell (an imprint of Cassell plc.), Artillery House, Artillery Row, London, SW1P 1RT, England; 1988.

FITCH, Charles Maden, *Fresh Flowers, Identifying, Selecting, and Arranging*, Abbeville Press, Inc., 488 Madison Avenue, New York, N.Y. 10022, USA; 1992.

NOVAK, Joanna and RUDNICKI, Ryszard M., *Postharvest Handling and Storage of Cut Flowers, Florist Greens, and Potted Plants*, Chapman and Hall, 11 New Fetter Lane, London, EC4P 4EE, England.

BRICKNELL, Christopher (Editor-in-chief), *The Royal Horticultural Society Gardener's Encyclopedia of Plants & Flowers*, Dorling Kindersley Publishers Ltd., 9 Henrietta Street, London, WC2 8PS, England; 1989.

Snijbloemen, Cut Flowers, Schnittblumen, Fleurs Coupees, Fiori da Vaso, Flores Cortadas. The Flower Council of Holland, Schipholweg 1, 2316 XB, Leiden, Holland; 1992.

ACKNOWLEDGMENTS

The publishers would like to thank the photographic agencies who have kindly supplied photographs for publication in this book:

© **Bruce Coleman**: Page 43 (*Campanula glomerata*), photography by R. Wanscheidt. Page 48 (*Centurea macrocephala*). Page 57 (*Cosmea glauca*), photographed by Eric Crichton. Page 67 (*Dimorphotheca aurantiaca*), photographed by Ron Boardman. Page 77 (*Galanthus nivalis*), photographed by Hans Reinhard. Page 90 (*Helleborus niger*), photographed by Hans Reinhard. Page 127 (*Paphiopedilum* hybrid), photographed by Kim Taylor. Page 135 (*Prunus persica*), photographed by Eric Crichton.

© **Photos Horticultural**: Page 45 (*Cattleya* hybrid). Page 113 (*Mahonia aquifolium* fruits and *Mahonia aquifolium* flowers). Page 171 (*Ilex aquifolium*). Page 175 (*Ruscus racemosus*).

© **Harry Smith**: Page 43 (*Campanula persicifolia*). Page 56 (*Coreopsis grandiflora* single form and *Coreopsis grandiflora* double form). Page 57 (*Cosmea sulphureus*). Page 61 (*Dahlia* hybrid – collarette, single flowered). Page 68 (*Doronicum* species). Page 78 (*Gardenia jasminoides*). Page 102 (*Lavatera trimestris*). Page 136 (*Prunus dulcis*). Page 163 (*Asparagus densiflorus myriocladus*). Page 165 (*Buxus sempervirens* – variegated). Page 165 (*Codiaeum variegatum pictum*). Page 167 (*Cyperus papyrus*).

The author would like to thank:

Tony Flavin of Baker & Duguid (Covent Garden) Ltd. for sourcing the best flowers in the market. **Veronica Richardson** of The Flowers & Plants Association for her expertise and encouragement. **James Hamilton** for his invaluable advice and patience.